HOMESTEAD COOKBOOK

MEGA BUNDLE – 7 Manuscripts in 1 – 300+ Homestead - friendly recipes for a balanced and healthy diet

TABLE OF CONTENTS

11

Introduction

Homestead recipes for personal enjoyment but also for family enjoyment. You will love them for sure for how easy it is to prepare them.

AVOCADO PANCAKES

Serves: **4**
Prep Time: **10**   Minutes

Cook Time: **20**   Minutes

Total Time: **30**   Minutes

INGREDIENTS

- 1 cup whole wheat flour
- ¼ tsp baking soda
- ¼ tsp baking powder
- 1 avocado
- 2 eggs
- 1 cup milk

DIRECTIONS

1. In a bowl combine all ingredients together and mix well
2. In a skillet heat olive oil
3. Pour ¼ of the batter and cook each pancake for 1-2 minutes per side
4. When ready remove from heat and serve

MUSHROOMS PANCAKES

Serves: **4**

Prep Time: **10** Minutes

Cook Time: **30** Minutes

Total Time: **40** Minutes

INGREDIENTS

- 1 cup whole wheat flour
- ¼ tsp baking soda
- ¼ tsp baking powder
- 1 cup mushrooms
- 2 eggs
- 1 cup milk

DIRECTIONS

1. In a bowl combine all ingredients together and mix well
2. In a skillet heat olive oil
3. Pour ¼ of the batter and cook each pancake for 1-2 minutes per side
4. When ready remove from heat and serve

BANANA PANCAKES

Serves: **4**
Prep Time: **10**   Minutes

Cook Time: **20**   Minutes

Total Time: **30**   Minutes

INGREDIENTS

- 1 cup whole wheat flour
- ¼ tsp baking soda
- ¼ tsp baking powder
- 1 cup mashed banana
- 2 eggs
- 1 cup milk

DIRECTIONS

1. In a bowl combine all ingredients together and mix well
2. In a skillet heat olive oil
3. Pour ¼ of the batter and cook each pancake for 1-2 minutes per side
4. When ready remove from heat and serve

Serves: **4**

Prep Time: **10**   Minutes

Cook Time: **20**   Minutes

Total Time: **30**   Minutes

INGREDIENTS

- 1 cup whole wheat flour
- ¼ tsp baking soda
- ¼ tsp baking powder
- 2 lime slices
- 2 eggs
- 1 cup milk

DIRECTIONS

1. In a bowl combine all ingredients together and mix well
2. In a skillet heat olive oil
3. Pour ¼ of the batter and cook each pancake for 1-2 minutes per side
4. When ready remove from heat and serve

SIMPLE PANCAKES

Serves: *4*
Prep Time: *10*   Minutes

Cook Time: *30*   Minutes

Total Time: *40*   Minutes

INGREDIENTS

- 1 cup whole wheat flour
- ¼ tsp baking soda
- ¼ tsp baking powder
- 2 eggs
- 1 cup milk

DIRECTIONS

1. In a bowl combine all ingredients together and mix well
2. In a skillet heat olive oil
3. Pour ¼ of the batter and cook each pancake for 1-2 minutes per side
4. When ready remove from heat and serve

GINGER MUFFINS

Serves: **8-12**
Prep Time: **10**   Minutes

Cook Time: **20**   Minutes

Total Time: **30**   Minutes

INGREDIENTS

- 2 eggs
- 1 tablespoon olive oil
- 1 cup milk
- 2 cups whole wheat flour
- 1 tsp baking soda
- ¼ tsp baking soda
- 1 tsp ginger
- 1 tsp cinnamon
- ¼ cup molasses

DIRECTIONS

1. In a bowl combine all wet ingredients
2. In another bowl combine all dry ingredients
3. Combine wet and dry ingredients together
4. Fold in ginger and mix well
5. Pour mixture into 8-12 prepared muffin cups, fill 2/3 of the cups

6. Bake for 18-20 minutes at 375 F
7. When ready remove from the oven and serve

LEMON MUFFINS

Serves: **8-12**

Prep Time: **10** Minutes

Cook Time: **20** Minutes

Total Time: **30** Minutes

INGREDIENTS

- 2 eggs
- 1 tablespoon olive oil
- 1 cup milk
- 2 cups whole wheat flour
- 1 tsp baking soda
- ¼ tsp baking soda
- Lemon slices
- 1 cup mashed banana

DIRECTIONS

1. In a bowl combine all wet ingredients
2. In another bowl combine all dry ingredients
3. Combine wet and dry ingredients together
4. Pour mixture into 8-12 prepared muffin cups, fill 2/3 of the cups
5. Bake for 18-20 minutes at 375 F
6. When ready remove from the oven and serve

BLUEBERRY MUFFINS

Serves: **8-12**
Prep Time: **10**   Minutes

Cook Time: **20**   Minutes

Total Time: **30**   Minutes

INGREDIENTS

- 2 eggs
- 1 tablespoon olive oil
- 1 cup milk
- 2 cups whole wheat flour
- 1 tsp baking soda
- ¼ tsp baking soda
- 1 tsp cinnamon
- 1 cup blueberries

DIRECTIONS

1. In a bowl combine all wet ingredients
2. In another bowl combine all dry ingredients
3. Combine wet and dry ingredients together
4. Fold in blueberries and mix well
5. Pour mixture into 8-12 prepared muffin cups, fill 2/3 of the cups
6. Bake for 18-20 minutes at 375 F, when ready remove and serve

MANGO MUFFINS

Serves: **8-12**

Prep Time: **10**   Minutes

Cook Time: **20**   Minutes

Total Time: **30**   Minutes

INGREDIENTS

- 2 eggs
- 1 tablespoon olive oil
- 1 cup milk
- 2 cups whole wheat flour
- 1 tsp baking soda
- ¼ tsp baking soda
- 1 tsp cinnamon
- 1 cup mango

DIRECTIONS

1. In a bowl combine all wet ingredients
2. In another bowl combine all dry ingredients
3. Combine wet and dry ingredients together
4. Pour mixture into 8-12 prepared muffin cups, fill 2/3 of the cups
5. Bake for 18-20 minutes at 375 F
6. When ready remove from the oven and serve

CHOCOLATE MUFFINS

Serves: *8-12*
Prep Time: *10*   Minutes

Cook Time: *20*   Minutes

Total Time: *30*   Minutes

INGREDIENTS

- 2 eggs
- 1 tablespoon olive oil
- 1 cup milk
- 2 cups whole wheat flour
- 1 tsp baking soda
- ¼ tsp baking soda
- 1 tsp cinnamon
- 1 cup chocolate chips

DIRECTIONS

1. In a bowl combine all wet ingredients
2. In another bowl combine all dry ingredients
3. Combine wet and dry ingredients together
4. Fold in chocolate chips and mix well
5. Pour mixture into 8-12 prepared muffin cups, fill 2/3 of the cups
6. Bake for 18-20 minutes at 375 F, when ready remove and serve

APRICOT MUFFINS

Serves: **8-12**

Prep Time: **10**   Minutes

Cook Time: **20**   Minutes

Total Time: **30**   Minutes

INGREDIENTS

- 2 eggs
- 1 tablespoon olive oil
- 1 cup milk
- 2 cups whole wheat flour
- 1 tsp baking soda
- ¼ tsp baking soda
- 1 cup apricots

DIRECTIONS

1. In a bowl combine all wet ingredients
2. In another bowl combine all dry ingredients
3. Combine wet and dry ingredients together
4. Pour mixture into 8-12 prepared muffin cups, fill 2/3 of the cups
5. Bake for 18-20 minutes at 375 F
6. When ready remove from the oven and serve

OMELETTE

Serves: *1*
Prep Time: 5   Minutes

Cook Time: *10*   Minutes

Total Time: *15*   Minutes

INGREDIENTS

- 2 eggs
- ¼ tsp salt
- ¼ tsp black pepper
- 1 tablespoon olive oil
- ¼ cup cheese
- ¼ tsp basil

DIRECTIONS

1. In a bowl combine all ingredients together and mix well
2. In a skillet heat olive oil and pour the egg mixture
3. Cook for 1-2 minutes per side
4. When ready remove omelette from the skillet and serve

Serves: *1*
Prep Time: 5   Minutes

Cook Time: *10* Minutes

Total Time: *15* Minutes

INGREDIENTS

- 2 eggs
- ¼ tsp salt
- ¼ tsp black pepper
- 1 tablespoon olive oil
- ¼ cup cheese
- ¼ tsp basil
- 1 cup mushrooms

DIRECTIONS

1. In a bowl combine all ingredients together and mix well
2. In a skillet heat olive oil and pour the egg mixture
3. Cook for 1-2 minutes per side
4. When ready remove omelette from the skillet and serve

CORN OMELETTE

Serves: *1*
Prep Time: *5*   Minutes

Cook Time: *10*   Minutes

Total Time: *15*   Minutes

INGREDIENTS

- 2 eggs
- ¼ tsp salt
- ¼ tsp black pepper
- 1 tablespoon olive oil
- ¼ cup cheese
- ¼ tsp basil
- 1 cup corn

DIRECTIONS

1. In a bowl combine all ingredients together and mix well
2. In a skillet heat olive oil and pour the egg mixture
3. Cook for 1-2 minutes per side
4. When ready remove omelette from the skillet and serve

BASIL OMELETTE

Serves: *1*
Prep Time: *5*   Minutes

Cook Time: *10*   Minutes

Total Time: *15*   Minutes

INGREDIENTS

- 2 eggs
- ¼ tsp salt
- ¼ tsp black pepper
- 1 tablespoon olive oil
- ¼ cup cheese
- ¼ tsp basil
- 1 cup mushrooms

DIRECTIONS

1. In a bowl combine all ingredients together and mix well
2. In a skillet heat olive oil and pour the egg mixture
3. Cook for 1-2 minutes per side
4. When ready remove omelette from the skillet and serve

TOMATO OMELETTE

Serves: *1*
Prep Time: *5*   Minutes
Cook Time: *10*   Minutes
Total Time: *15*   Minutes

INGREDIENTS

- 2 eggs
- ¼ tsp salt
- ¼ tsp black pepper
- 1 tablespoon olive oil
- ¼ cup cheese
- ¼ tsp basil
- 1 cup tomatoes

DIRECTIONS

1. In a bowl combine all ingredients together and mix well
2. In a skillet heat olive oil and pour the egg mixture
3. Cook for 1-2 minutes per side
4. When ready remove omelette from the skillet and serve

TUNA SANDWICH

Serves: **4**

Prep Time: **5**   Minutes

Cook Time: **5**   Minutes

Total Time: **10**   Minutes

INGREDIENTS

- 1 tablespoon mayonnaise
- ¼ tsp salt
- 2 bread slices
- 1 tuna tin

DIRECTIONS

1. Mix the tuna, mayonnaise and celery together then season
2. Toast the bread
3. Spread the tuna mixture over the bread and serve

Serves: **4**

Prep Time: **10**   Minutes

Cook Time: **10**   Minutes

Total Time: **20**   Minutes

INGREDIENTS

- 2-3 tbs oil
- 1 garlic clove
- Pepper
- 1 cup green beans
- 2 lb potatoes
- Salt
- 4 eggs

DIRECTIONS

1. Peel and dice the potatoes then boil until starting to soften
2. Dice the green beans and cook for almost 5 minutes then drain
3. Cook the potatoes in hot oil until crispy then add the green beans and the garlic

FRENCH TOAST

Serves: *4*
Prep Time: *10* Minutes

Cook Time: *20* Minutes

Total Time: *30* Minutes

INGREDIENTS

- 3 tbs honey
- 1 cup milk
- 4 slices of bread
- 2 eggs
- 2 tsp vanilla

DIRECTIONS

1. Preheat the oven to 350 F
2. Whisk together the milk, vanilla, eggs, and honey
3. Place the bread into a dish and pour the egg mixture over
4. Bake for at least 20 minutes
5. Serve drizzled with honey

Serves: *1*
Prep Time: *5*   Minutes

Cook Time: *5*   Minutes

Total Time: *10*   Minutes

INGREDIENTS

- Porridge
- Honey
- Blueberries
- Almonds
- 1 banana
- Chia seeds

DIRECTIONS

1. Mix everything together
2. Serve drizzled with honey

LUNCH

SPINACH FRITATTA

Serves: **2**

Prep Time: **10**   Minutes

Cook Time: **20**   Minutes

Total Time: **30**   Minutes

INGREDIENTS

- ½ lb. spinach
- 1 tablespoon olive oil
- ½ red onion
- 2 eggs
- ¼ tsp salt
- 2 oz. cheddar cheese
- 1 garlic clove
- ¼ tsp dill

DIRECTIONS

1. In a bowl whisk eggs with salt and cheese
2. In a frying pan heat olive oil and pour egg mixture
3. Add remaining ingredients and mix well
4. Serve when ready

TURNIP FRITATTA

Serves: **2**
Prep Time: **10** Minutes

Cook Time: **20** Minutes

Total Time: **30** Minutes

INGREDIENTS

- ½ lb. spinach
- ¼ cup turnip
- ½ red onion
- 2 eggs
- ¼ tsp salt
- 2 oz. cheddar cheese
- 1 garlic clove
- ¼ tsp dill

DIRECTIONS

1. In a bowl whisk eggs with salt and cheese
2. In a frying pan heat olive oil and pour egg mixture
3. Add remaining ingredients and mix well
4. Serve when ready

SQUASH FRITATTA

Serves: **2**

Prep Time: **10**   Minutes

Cook Time: **20**   Minutes

Total Time: **30**   Minutes

INGREDIENTS

- 1 cup squash
- 1 tablespoon olive oil
- ½ red onion
- 2 eggs
- ¼ tsp salt
- 2 oz. cheddar cheese
- 1 garlic clove
- ¼ tsp dill

DIRECTIONS

1. In a bowl whisk eggs with salt and cheese
2. In a frying pan heat olive oil and pour egg mixture
3. Add remaining ingredients and mix well
4. Serve when ready

HAM FRITATTA

Serves: **2**
Prep Time: **10**   Minutes

Cook Time: **20**   Minutes

Total Time: **30**   Minutes

INGREDIENTS

- 8-10 slices ham
- 1 tablespoon olive oil
- ½ red onion
- 2 eggs
- ¼ tsp salt
- 2 oz. parmesan cheese
- 1 garlic clove
- ¼ tsp dill

DIRECTIONS

1. In a bowl whisk eggs with salt and parmesan cheese
2. In a frying pan heat olive oil and pour egg mixture
3. Add remaining ingredients and mix well
4. When prosciutto and eggs are cooked remove from heat and serve

ONION FRITATTA

Serves: *2*
Prep Time: *10* Minutes

Cook Time: *20* Minutes

Total Time: *30* Minutes

INGREDIENTS

- 1 tablespoon olive oil
- ½ red onion
- 2 eggs
- ¼ tsp salt
- 2 oz. cheddar cheese
- 1 garlic clove
- ¼ tsp dill

DIRECTIONS

1. In a bowl whisk eggs with salt and cheese
2. In a frying pan heat olive oil and pour egg mixture
3. Add remaining ingredients and mix well
4. Serve when ready

FRIED CHICKEN WITH ALMONDS

Serves: *2*
Prep Time: *10*   Minutes

Cook Time: *25*   Minutes

Total Time: *35*   Minutes

INGREDIENTS

- 1 cup bread crumbs
- ¼ cup parmesan cheese
- ¼ cup almonds
- 1 tsp salt
- 1 tablespoon parley leaves
- 1 clove garlic
- ½ cup olive oil
- 2 lb. chicken breast

DIRECTIONS

1. In a bowl combine parsley, almonds, garlic, parmesan, bread crumbs, salt and mix well
2. In a bowl add olive oil and dip chicken breast into olive oil
3. Place chicken into the breadcrumb mixture and toss to coat
4. Bake chicken at 375 F for 20-25 minutes
5. When ready remove chicken from the oven and serve

FILET MIGNON WITH TOMATO SAUCE

Serves: **4**

Prep Time: **10** Minutes

Cook Time: **30** Minutes

Total Time: **40** Minutes

INGREDIENTS

- 1 tsp soy sauce
- 1 tsp mustard
- 1 tsp parsley leaves
- 1 clove garlic
- 2-3 tomatoes
- 2 tsp olive oil
- 4-5 beef tenderloin steaks
- ½ tsp salt

DIRECTIONS

1. In a bowl combine parsley, garlic, soy sauce, mustard and mix well
2. Stir in tomatoes slices and toss to coat
3. In a skillet heat olive oil and place the steak
4. Cook until golden brown for 3-4 minutes
5. Transfer skillet to the oven and bake at 375 F for 8-10 minutes
6. When ready remove and serve with tomato sauce

ZUCCHINI NOODLES

Serves: **1**

Prep Time: **5** Minutes

Cook Time: **15** Minutes

Total Time: **20** Minutes

INGREDIENTS

- 2 zucchinis
- 1 tablespoon olive oil
- 1 garlic clove
- ½ cup parmesan cheese
- 1 tsp salt

DIRECTIONS

1. Spiralize zucchini and set aside
2. In a skillet melt butter, add garlic and zucchini noodles
3. Toss to coat and cook for 5-6 minutes
4. When ready remove from the skillet and serve with parmesan cheese on top

GREEN BEANS WITH TOMATOES

Serves: **4**
Prep Time: **10** Minutes

Cook Time: **15** Minutes

Total Time: **25** Minutes

INGREDIENTS

- 1 cup water
- 1 lb. green beans
- 2 tomatoes
- 1 tsp olive oil
- 1 tsp Italian dressing
- salt

DIRECTIONS

1. In a pot bring water to a boil
2. Add green beans, tomatoes and boil for 10-12 minutes
3. Remove green beans and tomatoes to a bowl
4. Chop tomatoes, add Italian dressing, olive oil and serve

ROASTED CAULIFLOWER RICE

Serves: 2

Prep Time: *10* Minutes

Cook Time: 25 Minutes

Total Time: 35 Minutes

INGREDIENTS

- 3-4 cups frozen cauliflower rice
- 1 tablespoon olive oil
- 2 garlic cloves
- ½ cup parmesan cheese

DIRECTIONS

1. Place the cauliflower rice on a sheet pan
2. Sprinkle garlic and olive oil over the cauliflower rice and toss well
3. Spread cauliflower rice in a single layer in the pan
4. Roast cauliflower rice at 375 F for 20-25 minutes
5. When ready remove from the oven and serve with parmesan cheese on top

CAPRESE SALAD

Serves: 2
Prep Time: 5   Minutes

Cook Time: 5   Minutes

Total Time: *10*   Minutes

INGREDIENTS

- 3 cups tomatoes
- 2 oz. mozzarella cheese
- 2 tablespoons basil
- 1 tablespoon olive oil

DIRECTIONS

1. In a bowl mix all ingredients and mix well
2. Serve with dressing

Serves: **2**
Prep Time: **5** Minutes

Cook Time: **5** Minutes

Total Time: ***10*** Minutes

INGREDIENTS

- 3 cups butternut squash
- 1 cup cooked couscous
- 2 cups kale leaves
- 2 tablespoons cranberries
- 2 oz. goat cheese
- 1 cup salad dressing

DIRECTIONS

1. In a bowl mix all ingredients and mix well
2. Serve with dressing

TURKEY SALAD

Serves: 2
Prep Time: 5   Minutes

Cook Time: 5   Minutes

Total Time: *10* Minutes

INGREDIENTS

- 2 tablespoons lemon juice
- 2 tablespoons roasted garlic
- 2 tablespoons olive oil
- 1 tablespoon honey
- 2 cups cooked turkey breast
- 1 cup berries
- 1 cup green onions

DIRECTIONS

1. In a bowl mix all ingredients and mix well
2. Serve with dressing

SHRIMP SALAD

Serves:	*2*	
Prep Time:	5	Minutes
Cook Time:	5	Minutes
Total Time:	*10*	Minutes

INGREDIENTS

- 1 tsp cumin
- 1 tablespoon chili powder
- 1 tablespoon lemon juice
- 1 tsp garlic powder
- 1 cup corn
- 1 can beans
- 4 cups romaine lettuce
- 1 cup salsa
- 1 cup salad dressing

DIRECTIONS

1. In a bowl mix all ingredients and mix well
2. Serve with dressing

Serves: **2**
Prep Time: **5**   Minutes

Cook Time: **5**   Minutes

Total Time: **10**   Minutes

INGREDIENTS

- 2 cups watermelon
- 1 cup cantaloupe
- 1 tablespoon honey
- 1 tablespoon mint
- 1 tsp basil leaves
- ½ cup feta cheese

DIRECTIONS

1. In a bowl mix all ingredients and mix well
2. Serve with dressing

CORN SALAD

Serves: 2
Prep Time: 5   Minutes

Cook Time: 5   Minutes

Total Time: *10* Minutes

INGREDIENTS

- 1 cup corn
- 1 cup cucumber
- 1 cup tomatoes
- ¼ cup avocado
- 1 tablespoon lime juice
- ½ cup Greek yogurt
- 1 cup salad dressing

DIRECTIONS

1. In a bowl mix all ingredients and mix well
2. Serve with dressing

Serves: 2

Prep Time: 5   Minutes

Cook Time: 5   Minutes

Total Time: *10*   Minutes

INGREDIENTS

- 2 hard boiled eggs
- ¼ cup red onion
- 2 tablespoons capers
- 1 tablespoon lime juice
- 3 oz. smoked salmon
- 1 tablespoon olive oil

DIRECTIONS

1. In a bowl mix all ingredients and mix well
2. Serve with dressing

QUINOA SALAD

Serves: **2**
Prep Time: **5**   Minutes

Cook Time: **5**   Minutes

Total Time: **10**   Minutes

INGREDIENTS

- 1 cup cooked quinoa
- 1 tablespoon olive oil
- 1 tablespoon mustard
- 2 tablespoons lemon juice
- 1 cucumber
- ½ red onion
- ½ cup almonds
- 1 tablespoon mint

DIRECTIONS

1. In a bowl mix all ingredients and mix well
2. Serve with dressing

Serves: 2

Prep Time: 5   Minutes

Cook Time: 5   Minutes

Total Time: *10*   Minutes

INGREDIENTS

- 1 cup cucumber
- ¼ cup tomatoes
- ¼ cup red onion
- ¼ cup avocado
- ¼ cup feta cheese
- 1 tablespoon olives
- ¼ pecans
- 1 tablespoon vinegar
- 1 tsp olive oil

DIRECTIONS

1. In a bowl mix all ingredients and mix well
2. Serve with dressing

AVOCADO SALAD

Serves: 2
Prep Time: 5   Minutes

Cook Time: 5   Minutes

Total Time: 10   Minutes

INGREDIENTS

- 1 cup corn
- 1 cup tomatoes
- 1 cup cucumber
- ½ cup avocado
- ½ cup edamame
- 1 cup salad dressing

DIRECTIONS

1. In a bowl mix all ingredients and mix well
2. Serve with dressing

SIMPLE PIZZA RECIPE

Serves: **6-8**
Prep Time: **10**   Minutes

Cook Time: **15**   Minutes

Total Time: **25**   Minutes

INGREDIENTS

- 1 pizza crust
- ½ cup tomato sauce
- ¼ black pepper
- 1 cup pepperoni slices
- 1 cup mozzarella cheese
- 1 cup olives

DIRECTIONS

1. Spread tomato sauce on the pizza crust
2. Place all the toppings on the pizza crust
3. Bake the pizza at 425 F for 12-15 minutes
4. When ready remove pizza from the oven and serve

ZUCCHINI PIZZA

Serves: **6-8**

Prep Time: **10**   Minutes

Cook Time: **15**   Minutes

Total Time: **25**   Minutes

INGREDIENTS

- 1 pizza crust
- ½ cup tomato sauce
- ¼ black pepper
- 1 cup zucchini slices
- 1 cup mozzarella cheese
- 1 cup olives

DIRECTIONS

1. Spread tomato sauce on the pizza crust
2. Place all the toppings on the pizza crust
3. Bake the pizza at 425 F for 12-15 minutes
4. When ready remove pizza from the oven and serve

Serves: *6-8*

Prep Time: *10*   Minutes

Cook Time: *15*   Minutes

Total Time: *25*   Minutes

INGREDIENTS

- 1 pizza crust
- ½ cup tomato sauce
- ¼ black pepper
- 1 cup cauliflower
- 1 cup mozzarella cheese
- 1 cup olives

DIRECTIONS

1. Spread tomato sauce on the pizza crust
2. Place all the toppings on the pizza crust
3. Bake the pizza at 425 F for 12-15 minutes
4. When ready remove pizza from the oven and serve

Serves: **6-8**
Prep Time: **10**   Minutes

Cook Time: **15**   Minutes

Total Time: **25**   Minutes

INGREDIENTS

- 1 pizza crust
- ½ cup tomato sauce
- ¼ black pepper
- 1 cup broccoli
- 1 cup mozzarella cheese
- 1 cup olives

DIRECTIONS

1. Spread tomato sauce on the pizza crust
2. Place all the toppings on the pizza crust
3. Bake the pizza at 425 F for 12-15 minutes
4. When ready remove pizza from the oven and serve

TOMATOES & HAM PIZZA

Serves: **6-8**

Prep Time: **10**   Minutes

Cook Time: **15**   Minutes

Total Time: **25**   Minutes

INGREDIENTS

- 1 pizza crust
- ½ cup tomato sauce
- ¼ black pepper
- 1 cup pepperoni slices
- 1 cup tomatoes
- 6-8 ham slices
- 1 cup mozzarella cheese
- 1 cup olives

DIRECTIONS

1. Spread tomato sauce on the pizza crust
2. Place all the toppings on the pizza crust
3. Bake the pizza at 425 F for 12-15 minutes
4. When ready remove pizza from the oven and serve

LEEK SOUP

Serves: *4*

Prep Time: *10*   Minutes

Cook Time: *20*   Minutes

Total Time: *30*   Minutes

INGREDIENTS

- 1 tablespoon olive oil
- 1 lb. leek
- ¼ red onion
- ½ cup all-purpose flour
- ¼ tsp salt
- ¼ tsp pepper
- 1 can vegetable broth
- 1 cup heavy cream

DIRECTIONS

1. In a saucepan heat olive oil and sauté onion until tender
2. Add remaining ingredients to the saucepan and bring to a boil
3. When all the vegetables are tender transfer to a blender and blend until smooth
4. Pour soup into bowls, garnish with parsley and serve

ZUCCHINI SOUP

Serves: **4**
Prep Time: **10** Minutes

Cook Time: **20** Minutes

Total Time: **30** Minutes

INGREDIENTS

- 1 tablespoon olive oil
- 1 lb. zucchini
- ¼ red onion
- ½ cup all-purpose flour
- ¼ tsp salt
- ¼ tsp pepper
- 1 can vegetable broth
- 1 cup heavy cream

DIRECTIONS

1. In a saucepan heat olive oil and sauté zucchini until tender
2. Add remaining ingredients to the saucepan and bring to a boil
3. When all the vegetables are tender transfer to a blender and blend until smooth
4. Pour soup into bowls, garnish with parsley and serve

RUTABAGA SOUP

Serves: **4**

Prep Time: **10**   Minutes

Cook Time: **20**   Minutes

Total Time: **30**   Minutes

INGREDIENTS

- 1 tablespoon olive oil
- 1 lb. rutabaga
- ¼ red onion
- ½ cup all-purpose flour
- ¼ tsp salt
- ¼ tsp pepper
- 1 can vegetable broth
- 1 cup heavy cream

DIRECTIONS

1. In a saucepan heat olive oil and sauté onion until tender
2. Add remaining ingredients to the saucepan and bring to a boil
3. When all the vegetables are tender transfer to a blender and blend until smooth
4. Pour soup into bowls, garnish with parsley and serve

CARROT SOUP

Serves: *4*
Prep Time: *10* Minutes

Cook Time: *20* Minutes

Total Time: *30* Minutes

INGREDIENTS

- 1 tablespoon olive oil
- 1 lb. carrots
- ¼ red onion
- ½ cup all-purpose flour
- ¼ tsp salt
- ¼ tsp pepper
- 1 can vegetable broth
- 1 cup heavy cream

DIRECTIONS

1. In a saucepan heat olive oil and sauté carrots until tender
2. Add remaining ingredients to the saucepan and bring to a boil
3. When all the vegetables are tender transfer to a blender and blend until smooth
4. Pour soup into bowls, garnish with parsley and serve

YAMS SOUP

Serves: **4**
Prep Time: **10**   Minutes

Cook Time: **20**   Minutes

Total Time: **30**   Minutes

INGREDIENTS

- 1 tablespoon olive oil
- 1 lb. yams
- ¼ red onion
- ½ cup all-purpose flour
- ¼ tsp salt
- ¼ tsp pepper
- 1 can vegetable broth
- 1 cup heavy cream

DIRECTIONS

1. In a saucepan heat olive oil and sauté onion until tender
2. Add remaining ingredients to the saucepan and bring to a boil
3. When all the vegetables are tender transfer to a blender and blend until smooth
4. Pour soup into bowls, garnish with parsley and serve

SMOOTHIES

APPLE-GINGER SMOOTHIE

Serves: *1*
Prep Time: *5*   Minutes

Cook Time: *5*   Minutes

Total Time: *10* Minutes

INGREDIENTS

- 1 apple
- 1 cup almond milk
- 1 cup kale
- 1 tsp ginger

DIRECTIONS

1. In a blender place all ingredients and blend until smooth
2. Pour smoothie in a glass and serve

POMEGRANATE SMOOTHIE

Serves: *1*
Prep Time: 5   Minutes
Cook Time: 5   Minutes

Total Time: *10*   Minutes

INGREDIENTS

- 1 cucumber
- 1 pomegranate
- 1 cup ice
- 1 cup almond milk

DIRECTIONS

1. In a blender place all ingredients and blend until smooth
2. Pour smoothie in a glass and serve

Serves: *1*
Prep Time: 5   Minutes

Cook Time: 5   Minutes

Total Time: *10*   Minutes

INGREDIENTS

- 1 mango
- 1 cup strawberries
- 1 cup coconut milk
- 1 cup ice

DIRECTIONS

1. In a blender place all ingredients and blend until smooth
2. Pour smoothie in a glass and serve

CARAMEL SMOOTHIE

Serves: *1*
Prep Time: 5   Minutes

Cook Time: 5   Minutes

Total Time: *10*   Minutes

INGREDIENTS

- 1 cup caramel powder
- 1 cup almond milk
- 1 tsp cinnamon

DIRECTIONS

1. In a blender place all ingredients and blend until smooth
2. Pour smoothie in a glass and serve

BASIL SMOOTHIE

Serves: **1**

Prep Time: **5**   Minutes

Cook Time: **5**   Minutes

Total Time: **10**   Minutes

INGREDIENTS

- 1 cup blueberries
- 1 cup water
- 2 basil leaves
- ½ cup coconut milk
- 1 tablespoon peanut butter

DIRECTIONS

1. In a blender place all ingredients and blend until smooth
2. Pour smoothie in a glass and serve

PROTEIN SMOOTHIE

Serves: *1*
Prep Time: 5   Minutes

Cook Time: 5   Minutes

Total Time: *10* Minutes

INGREDIENTS

- 1 cup blueberries
- 1 cup cauliflower
- 1 cup vanilla yoghurt
- 1 cup protein powder

DIRECTIONS

1. In a blender place all ingredients and blend until smooth
2. Pour smoothie in a glass and serve

Serves: *1*
Prep Time: 5   Minutes

Cook Time: 5   Minutes

Total Time: *10* Minutes

INGREDIENTS

- 1 nectarine
- 2 oz. cauliflower
- 2 oz. swiss chard
- 1 tablespoon almond butter

DIRECTIONS

1. In a blender place all ingredients and blend until smooth
2. Pour smoothie in a glass and serve

GREEN LOW-CALORIE SMOOTHIE

Serves: *1*

Prep Time: 5   Minutes

Cook Time: 5   Minutes

Total Time: *10*   Minutes

INGREDIENTS

- 2 oz. baby spinach
- 1 cucumber
- 1 apple
- ¼ avocado
- 1 tsp ginger

DIRECTIONS

1. In a blender place all ingredients and blend until smooth
2. Pour smoothie in a glass and serve

RED SMOOTHIE

Serves: *1*
Prep Time: 5   Minutes

Cook Time: 5   Minutes

Total Time: *10* Minutes

INGREDIENTS

- 2 carrots
- 1 red beet
- ½ tomato
- One handful of watercress
- ½ cup ice

DIRECTIONS

1. In a blender place all ingredients and blend until smooth
2. Pour smoothie in a glass and serve

Serves: **1**
Prep Time: **5**   Minutes

Cook Time: **5**   Minutes

Total Time: **10**   Minutes

INGREDIENTS

- 1 cup broccoli
- 2 celery sticks
- 1 fennel bulb
- 1 cucumber
- 1 cup ice

DIRECTIONS

1. In a blender place all ingredients and blend until smooth
2. Pour smoothie in a glass and serve

SECOND COOKBOOK

ROASTED CHERRY & RICOTTA TARTINE

Serves: **2**
Prep Time: **20**   Minutes

Cook Time: **30**   Minutes

Total Time: **50**   Minutes

INGREDIENTS

- 2 cups cherries
- 1 tablespoon honey
- 1 tsp lemon zest
- 1 tablespoon lemon juice
- 1 tsp olive oil
- salt
- 4 slices bread
- 1 cup part-skim ricotta cheese
- 1 tsp thyme
- ½ cup almonds

DIRECTIONS

1. Preheat the oven to 375 F
2. In a bowl toss with lemon juice, oil, honey and roast them for about 12-15 minutes

3. Toast bread and top with lemon zest, ricotta cheese, cherries, thyme, almonds, and salt
4. Drizzle with honey and serve

Serves: **4**

Prep Time: **10** Minutes

Cook Time: **10** Minutes

Total Time: **20** Minutes

INGREDIENTS

- ½ cup mango
- ¼ cup Greek Yogurt
- ½ cup banana
- ½ cup unsweetened almond milk
- 4 tablespoons almonds
- ½ tsp allspice
- ½ cup raspberries
- ¼ tsp honey

DIRECTIONS

1. In a blender add all ingredients and blend until smooth
2. Pour the mango yogurt into a bowl and serve with raspberries and almonds

Serves: **4**

Prep Time: **10** Minutes

Cook Time: **30** Minutes

Total Time: **40** Minutes

INGREDIENTS

- 1 oz. ham
- 1 oz. turkey
- 1 oz. Swiss cheese
- 1 egg
- 3 leaves romaine lettuce
- ½ cup yellow bell pepper
- ½ cup red onion
- ½ cup cucumber
- 1 tomato
- 1 carrot
- 1 tablespoon salad dressing
- 2 large tomato wraps

DIRECTIONS

1. Roll ham, turkey and Swiss cheese and cut into thin strips, toss with vegetables and roll your tortilla
2. Place a tablespoon of dressing on your tortilla

CHOCOLATE OAT BARS

Serves: *4*
Prep Time: *10* Minutes

Cook Time: *30* Minutes

Total Time: *40* Minutes

INGREDIENTS

- 1 egg
- ¼ cup yogurt
- ¼ cup brown sugar
- 1 cup quick oats
- 1 tablespoon flaxseed
- ½ cup chocolate chips

DIRECTIONS

1. In a bowl whisk yogurt, egg, and sugar
2. In a blender add oats, flaxseed, chocolate chips, egg mixture and blend until smooth
3. Spread mixture in a pan and bake at 325 F for 25 min
4. Remove, cut into bars and serve

RICE PUDDING

Serves: **4**

Prep Time: **10**   Minutes

Cook Time: **30**   Minutes

Total Time: **40**   Minutes

INGREDIENTS

- 2 cups water
- 1 cup brown rice
- 1 cup milk
- 1 cup Splenda
- 1 cup crystallized ginger

DIRECTIONS

1. In a saucepan bring water and rice to a boil, reduce heat and cook for 25-30 minutes
2. Stir in Splenda while rice is cooking
3. Add milk, ginger and spend and cook until milk is absorbed
4. Remove from heat garnish with orange slices and serve

LEMON MERINGUE

Serves: *3*
Prep Time: *10*   Minutes

Cook Time: *35*   Minutes

Total Time: *45*   Minutes

INGREDIENTS

- 2 egg whites
- ½ cup Splenda
- ½ tsp vanilla
- 1 tablespoon lemon curd

DIRECTIONS

1. In a bowl beat egg whites, add Splenda and continue to mix
2. Stir in vanilla and mix well
3. Drop mixture using a pipe onto a baking sheet making around 10-12 portions
4. Bake at 275 F for 25-30 minutes
5. Remove and serve

LEMONADE

Serves: **2**
Prep Time: **10**   Minutes

Cook Time: **10**   Minutes

Total Time: **20**   Minutes

INGREDIENTS

- 1 lemon
- 1 packet sweet
- 1 cup water
- 1 cup ice cubes

DIRECTIONS

1. Cut lemon in half and squeeze the juice into a glass
2. Add sweetener, water, and ice cubes
3. Mix well, garnish with a strawberry and serve

Serves: *8*
Prep Time: *10*   Minutes

Cook Time: *35*   Minutes

Total Time: *45*   Minutes

INGREDIENTS

- 1 15 oz. can pumpkin
- ½ cup egg substitute
- ¾ cup sugar
- 1 tsp cinnamon
- ¼ tsp ground ginger
- ½ tsp nutmeg
- ½ tsp cloves
- 1 12 oz. can evaporated skim milk

CRUST

- 1 cup flour
- 2 tablespoons water
- ½ cup shortening

DIRECTIONS

1. Preheat the oven to 400 F

2. Place shortening, water, and flour into a bowl and mix well and form a ball

3. Let it stand for 20-30 minutes and then roll crust in a pan

4. In a whisk together pumpkin, sugar, egg substitute, evaporated milk and mix well

5. Pour mixture into pie shell and bake for 35 minutes

6. Remove and serve

FRUIT TARTS

Serves: **2**
Prep Time: **10** Minutes

Cook Time: **20** Minutes

Total Time: **30** Minutes

INGREDIENTS

- 1 tart apple
- 1 tablespoon Splenda
- ½ tsp cinnamon
- 10 wonton wrappers

DIRECTIONS

1. Preheat the oven to 325 F
2. Grate the apples and sprinkle with cinnamon and Splenda
3. Fill a muffin pan with grated apple and bake for 10-12 minutes, remove and serve

Serves: **1**

Prep Time: **10** Minutes

Cook Time: **10** Minutes

Total Time: **20** Minutes

INGREDIENTS

- 3 cups cold water
- 2 peaches tea bags
- 1 cup ice cubes

DIRECTIONS

1. **Pour water, ice cubes and tea bags in a glass**
2. **After 2-3 minutes remove tea bags and serve**

Serves: *4*

Prep Time: *10*   Minutes

Cook Time: *30*   Minutes

Total Time: *40*   Minutes

INGREDIENTS

- 1 kiwi
- ½ cup strawberries
- ¾ seltzer
- 1 cup ice cubes

DIRECTIONS

1. In a bowl mash kiwi and strawberries
2. Pour juice, ice, and top with seltzer
3. Mix well and serve

Serves: **4**
Prep Time: **10**   Minutes

Cook Time: **10**   Minutes

Total Time: **20**   Minutes

INGREDIENTS

- ½ cup ketchup
- ½ cup oil
- ½ cup white vinegar
- 1 tsp lemon juice
- 4 bread slices

DIRECTIONS

1. In a bowl stir all ingredients until well combined
2. Dip the bread into the mixture
3. Fry bread for 1-2 minutes per side
4. Remove and serve

Serves: **4**
Prep Time: **10**   Minutes

Cook Time: **30**   Minutes

Total Time: **40**   Minutes

INGREDIENTS

- 1 cup dark rum
- 1 tsp lemon rind
- ¾ cup artificial sweetener
- 1 cup walnuts
- 1 cup pecans
- 3 cups cranberries

DIRECTIONS

1. In a saucepan add Splenda, rum and bring to a boil
2. Add cranberries, lemon zest and simmer on low heat for 12-15 minutes
3. Add nuts cook for 2-3 minutes, remove and serve

BANANA SPLIT

Serves: **2**

Prep Time: **10** Minutes

Cook Time: **10** Minutes

Total Time: **20** Minutes

INGREDIENTS

- 2 bananas
- 1 cup strawberries
- 1 cup blackberries
- 1 cup chopped pineapple
- 1 cup coconut milk
- 1 tablespoon whole grain granola
- ¼ ounce roasted coconut chips

DIRECTIONS

1. Slice the bananas and place them into a bowl
2. Divide the strawberries, blackberries, and pineapple and place it in the bottom of the bowl
3. Top with yogurt and divide the granola and coconut chips between the bananas

CHAI-SPICED PEAR OATMEAL

Serves: 2

Prep Time: *10*   Minutes

Cook Time: *30*   Minutes

Total Time: *40*   Minutes

INGREDIENTS

- 1 cup oats
- ½ tsp ground cinnamon
- 1 tsp maple syrup
- 1 tablespoon walnut halves
- 2 tsp coconut oil
- 1 Anjou pear spiralized
- 1 cup almond milk
- ½ tsp vanilla extract

DIRECTIONS

1. In a saucepan boil water and add oats for another 10 minutes
2. In a skillet heat coconut oil over medium heat and add almond milk, pear noodles, cinnamon, maple syrup, and vanilla extract
3. Stir to simmer for about 10-15 minutes
4. In another skillet place walnuts and cook for 5-6 minutes, remove from the pan when ready

5. Place the oatmeal in a bowl and top with pear mixture and toasted walnuts

POHA WAFFLES

Serves: **4**

Prep Time: **10** Minutes

Cook Time: **10** Minutes

Total Time: **20** Minutes

INGREDIENTS

- ½ cup rice flour
- 1 tsp baking soda
- 1 banana
- ½ tsp salt
- 2 tablespoons oil
- ½ cup milk
- 1 tsp cider vinegar
- 1 egg
- ½ cup quinoa flakes
- 1 tablespoon honey

DIRECTIONS

1. In a bowl mix all dry ingredients
2. Separate egg yolk from egg white and beat egg whites
3. Mix egg yolk with milk, honey, wet fruit and add dry ingredients to mixture
4. Add cider vinegar and mix gently

5. Pour mixture into waffle iron
6. When ready remove and serve

Serves: **12**

Prep Time: **10** Minutes

Cook Time: **15** Minutes

Total Time: **25** Minutes

INGREDIENTS

- 2 cups flour
- 1 tsp xantham gum
- ½ tsp salt
- 4 tablespoons margarine
- 1 tablespoon baking powder
- 1 tsp sugar

DIRECTIONS

1. Preheat oven to 425 F
2. Toss together all ingredients, gather into a ball
3. Form small biscuits and bake for 12-15 minutes
4. Remove and serve

Serves: *1*
Prep Time: *5*   Minutes

Cook Time: *10*   Minutes

Total Time: *15*   Minutes

INGREDIENTS

- 2 eggs
- ¼ tsp salt
- ¼ tsp black pepper
- 1 tablespoon olive oil
- ¼ cup cheese
- ¼ tsp basil
- 1 cup mushrooms

DIRECTIONS

1. In a bowl combine all ingredients together and mix well
2. In a skillet heat olive oil and pour the egg mixture
3. Cook for 1-2 minutes per side
4. When ready remove omelette from the skillet and serve

CABBAGE OMELETTE

Serves: *1*

Prep Time: *5*   Minutes

Cook Time: *10*   Minutes

Total Time: *15*   Minutes

INGREDIENTS

- 2 eggs
- 1 cup cabbage
- 1 cup cheese
- 1 tsp salt

DIRECTIONS

1. In a bowl combine all ingredients together and mix well
2. In a skillet heat olive oil and pour the egg mixture
3. Cook for 1-2 minutes per side
4. When ready remove omelette from the skillet and serve

TOASTED OATMEAL WITH SPICES

Serves: **2**

Prep Time: **5**   Minutes

Cook Time: **10** Minutes

Total Time: **15** Minutes

INGREDIENTS

- 1 cup gluten- free oats
- 2 cup water
- 1 cup unsweetened coconut
- 1 tsp vanilla extract
- ¼ tsp cinnamon
- ¼ tsp nutmeg
- 1 tablespoon coconut oil
- 1 apple
- 1 tablespoon maple syrup

DIRECTIONS

1. In a saucepan heat coconut oil, add oats and coconut flakes and toast for 2-3 minutes
2. Add water, milk, vanilla, nutmeg and stir
3. Serve with apple slices, cinnamon and maple syrup

PANCAKES

BANANA PANCAKES

Serves: *4*
Prep Time: *10*   Minutes

Cook Time: *20*   Minutes

Total Time: *30*   Minutes

INGREDIENTS

- 1 cup whole wheat flour
- ¼ tsp baking soda
- ¼ tsp baking powder
- 1 cup mashed banana
- 2 eggs
- 1 cup milk

DIRECTIONS

1. In a bowl combine all ingredients together and mix well
2. In a skillet heat olive oil
3. Pour ¼ of the batter and cook each pancake for 1-2 minutes per side
4. When ready remove from heat and serve

APPLE PANCAKES

Serves: **6**

Prep Time: **5**   Minutes

Cook Time: **10** Minutes

Total Time: **15** Minutes

INGREDIENTS

- 1 apple
- 1 cup almond flour
- ¼ tsp baking powder
- ¼ tsp salt
- 2 eggs
- 1 tablespoon olive oil

DIRECTIONS

1. In a bowl combine all ingredients together
2. In a skillet heat olive oil and pour 1/6 batter
3. Cook for 1-2 minutes per side
4. When ready remove from the skillet and serve

SMOOTHIES

BANANA SMOOTHIE

Serves: *1*

Prep Time: *5*   Minutes

Cook Time: *5*   Minutes

Total Time: *10*   Minutes

INGREDIENTS

- ¼ cup strawberries
- ½ banana
- 1 orange
- 1 cup ice

DIRECTIONS

1. In a blender place all ingredients and blend until smooth
2. Pour smoothie in a glass and serve

BLUEBERRY DETOX SMOOTHIE

Serves: *1*
Prep Time: *5* Minutes

Cook Time: *5* Minutes

Total Time: *10* Minutes

INGREDIENTS

- 1 banana
- 1 handful of blueberries
- 1 tablespoon coconut oil
- 1 tablespoon hemp seeds
- 1 tablespoon chia seeds
- pinch of cinnamon

DIRECTIONS

1. In a blender place all ingredients and blend until smooth
2. Pour smoothie in a glass and serve

Serves: *1*
Prep Time: 5   Minutes

Cook Time: 5   Minutes

Total Time: *10* Minutes

INGREDIENTS

- ¼ cucumber
- 1 cup blueberries
- 6 oz. coconut water
- 1 tablespoon chia seeds
- 1 tablespoon honey
- ice cubes

DIRECTIONS

1. In a blender place all ingredients and blend until smooth
2. Pour smoothie in a glass and serve

CRANBERRY DETOX SMOOTHIE

Serves: *1*
Prep Time: 5   Minutes

Cook Time: 5   Minutes

Total Time: *10*   Minutes

INGREDIENTS

- 1 cup mixed berries
- ½ cup cranberry juice
- ½ avocado
- 1 cup coconut water
- 1 tablespoon chia seeds
- 1 tsp ginger

DIRECTIONS

1. In a blender place all ingredients and blend until smooth
2. Pour smoothie in a glass and serve

PUMPKIN SMOOTHIE

Serves: *1*
Prep Time: *5*   Minutes

Cook Time: *5*   Minutes

Total Time: *10* Minutes

INGREDIENTS

- ½ cup pumpkin
- ½ cup coconut milk
- 1 tablespoon chia seeds
- ½ cup coconut water
- 1 tsp honey
- 1 tsp cinnamon
- ¼ tsp nutmeg
- ¼ tsp pumpkin pie spice

DIRECTIONS

1. In a blender place all ingredients and blend until smooth
2. Pour smoothie in a glass and serve

CINNAMON-BLACKBERRY SMOOTHIE

Serves: **1**

Prep Time: **5** Minutes

Cook Time: **5** Minutes

Total Time: **10** Minutes

INGREDIENTS

- 1 cup blackberries
- 1 cup coconut water
- 1 tablespoon chia seeds
- ¼ tsp cinnamon
- 1 handful spinach
- 1 tablespoon honey

DIRECTIONS

1. In a blender place all ingredients and blend until smooth
2. Pour smoothie in a glass and serve

KALE LIVER DETOX SMOOTHIE

Serves: *1*
Prep Time: 5   Minutes

Cook Time: 5   Minutes

Total Time: *10*   Minutes

INGREDIENTS

- 1 cup Kale
- 1 apple
- 1 lemon
- 1-inch ginger
- 1 cup water

DIRECTIONS

1. In a blender place all ingredients and blend until smooth
2. Pour smoothie in a glass and serve

GREEN DETOX SMOOTHIE

Serves: **1**
Prep Time: **5** Minutes

Cook Time: **5** Minutes

Total Time: **10** Minutes

INGREDIENTS

- 1 cup coconut water
- 1 handful kale
- 1 handful spinach
- 4 stalks celery
- 1 apple
- juice of 1 lemon
- ¼ bunch parsley

DIRECTIONS

1. In a blender place all ingredients and blend until smooth
2. Pour smoothie in a glass and serve

COOKIES

BANANA COOKIES

Serves: *8*
Prep Time: *10*   Minutes

Cook Time: *10*   Minutes

Total Time: *20*   Minutes

INGREDIENTS

- 2 medjool dates
- ¼ cup butter
- ¼ cup desiccated coconut
- ¼ cup walnuts
- 2 tablespoons banana flour
- Stevia extract
- ¼ tsp cinnamon

DIRECTIONS

1. In a blender add all ingredients and blend until smooth
2. Remove from the blender and roll into balls
3. Sprinkle with coconut and refrigerate
4. When ready remove from the fridge and serve

Serves: *8-12*
Prep Time: 5   Minutes

Cook Time: 15   Minutes

Total Time: *20*   Minutes

INGREDIENTS

- 1 cup rolled oats
- ¼ cup applesauce
- ½ tsp vanilla extract
- 3 tablespoons chocolate chips
- 2 tablespoons dried fruits
- 1 tsp cinnamon

DIRECTIONS

1. Preheat the oven to 325 F
2. In a bowl combine all ingredients together and mix well
3. Scoop cookies using an ice cream scoop
4. Place cookies onto a prepared baking sheet
5. Place in the oven for 12-15 minutes or until the cookies are done
6. When ready remove from the oven and serve

BROWNIE COOKIES

Serves: **4**

Prep Time: **10** Minutes

Cook Time: **30** Minutes

Total Time: **40** Minutes

INGREDIENTS

- 2 oz. unsweetened chocolate
- 1 stick butter
- 1 cup Splenda
- 1 egg
- ¼ tsp vanilla
- ¾ cup whole-wheat flour
- ½ tsp baking soda
- ¼ cup chocolate chips
- ¼ cup walnuts

DIRECTIONS

1. Preheat the oven to 325 F
2. Microwave chocolate for 30 seconds
3. In another bowl mix Splenda, butter, vanilla, and the egg
4. Stir in melted chocolate, baking soda, flour, chocolate chips, and nuts

5. Drop teaspoons of batter onto the baking sheet and bake for 10-12 minutes

6. Remove and serve

MUFFINS

SIMPLE MUFFINS

Serves: **8-12**

Prep Time: **10** Minutes

Cook Time: **20** Minutes

Total Time: **30** Minutes

INGREDIENTS

- 2 eggs
- 1 tablespoon olive oil
- 1 cup milk
- 2 cups whole wheat flour
- 1 tsp baking soda
- ¼ tsp baking soda
- 1 cup pumpkin puree
- 1 tsp cinnamon
- ¼ cup molasses

DIRECTIONS

1. In a bowl combine all dry ingredients
2. In another bowl combine all dry ingredients
3. Combine wet and dry ingredients together
4. Pour mixture into 8-12 prepared muffin cups, fill 2/3 of the cups

5. Bake for 18-20 minutes at 375 F

6. When ready remove from the oven and serve

ZUCCHINI MUFFINS

Serves: *8*

Prep Time: *10*   Minutes

Cook Time: *30*   Minutes

Total Time: *40*   Minutes

INGREDIENTS

- 2 cups almond flour
- 1 tsp baking powder
- 1 zucchini
- 1 tablespoon flaxseed
- 1 tablespoon honey
- 1 tsp oregano

DIRECTIONS

1. In a bowl combine water and flaxseed meal
2. Add all dry and wet ingredients, mix well
3. Pour mixture into 8-10 muffin cups
4. Bake for 20-25 minutes at 400 F
5. When ready remove and serve

CHOCOLATE MUFFINS

Serves: **8**
Prep Time: **10** Minutes

Cook Time: **30** Minutes

Total Time: **40** Minutes

INGREDIENTS

- 2 cups rice flour
- ¼ cup cornmeal
- 1 tablespoon baking powder
- ¼ tsp salt
- ¼ tsp nutmeg
- ¼ tsp chili powder
- ¼ cup cocoa powder
- 1 tablespoon flaxseed meal
- ¼ cup honey
- ¼ cup almond milk
- ¼ cup coconut oil
- ¼ cup olive oil

DIRECTIONS

1. In a bowl combine water and flaxseed meal
2. Add all dry and wet ingredients, mix well

3. Pour mixture into 8-10 muffin cups
4. Bake for 20-25 minutes at 400 F
5. When ready remove and serve

POTATO MUFFINS

Serves: *8*
Prep Time: *15* Minutes

Cook Time: *35* Minutes

Total Time: *50* Minutes

INGREDIENTS

- 2 tablespoons flaxseed
- ¼ cup water
- 1 cup sweet potato
- 1 cup apple sauce
- ¼ cup ghee
- 1 tablespoon maple syrup
- 1 cup rice flour
- 1 tsp baking powder
- 2 tsp chai mix
- 1 tsp salt

DIRECTIONS

1. In a bowl combine water and flaxseed meal
2. Add all dry and wet ingredients, mix well
3. Pour mixture into 8-10 muffin cups
4. Bake for 20-25 minutes at 400 F, when ready remove and serve

COCONUT MUFFINS

Serves: *4*

Prep Time: *10*   Minutes

Cook Time: *30*   Minutes

Total Time: *40*   Minutes

INGREDIENTS

- 2 bananas
- 1 tablespoon olive oil
- ¼ tsp baking powder
- ¼ tsp salt
- ½ cup coconut flour
- 1 tablespoon coconut flakes

DIRECTIONS

1. In a bowl combine wet and dry ingredients together and mix well
2. Pour mixture into 8-10 muffin cups
3. Bake for 20-25 minutes at 400 F
4. When ready remove and serve

OATMEAL MUFFINS

Serves: **8**

Prep Time: **10** Minutes

Cook Time: **20** Minutes

Total Time: **30** Minutes

INGREDIENTS

- 1 cup oats
- 1 cup flour
- 1 tsp baking powder
- ½ tsp salt
- ¾ cup brown sugar
- 1 egg
- 1 cup skim milk
- 1/2 cup vegetable oil
- 1 carrot
- 1 cup raisins
- ¼ cup walnuts

DIRECTIONS

1. Preheat the oven to 375 F
2. In a bowl mix flour, oats, salt, baking powder, and sugar
3. In another bowl beat eggs and carrots, vegetable oil and milk

4. Stir wet ingredients into dry ingredients and mix well
5. Stir in walnuts raisins and divide batter into 8-10 muffin cups
6. Bake for 18-20 minutes, remove and serve

THIRD COOKBOOK

ZUCCHINI APPLE PANCAKES

Serves: *4*

Prep Time: *10*   minutes

Cook Time: *10*   minutes

Total Time: *20*   minutes

INGREDIENTS

- 1 zucchini
- 2 tablespoons almond butter
- 2 eggs
- 1 tablespoon honey
- 2 tablespoons coconut oil
- 1 apple
- 1 cup almond flour
- ¼ tsp baking powder
- ¼ tsp sea salt

DIRECTIONS

1. Mix zucchini, honey, apples, thyme and almond butter in a bowl
2. In another bowl mix salt, baking powder and flour and beat the eggs
3. Mix all the ingredients from the bowl and heat coconut oil in a fry pan

4. Pour the mixture in the pan and cook for 1-2 minutes each side

QUINOA AND GOJI BERRIES

Serves: *4*
Prep Time: *5*   Minutes

Cook Time: *10* Minutes

Total Time: *15* Minutes

INGREDIENTS

- 1 cup quinoa
- 1 cup goji
- parsley as needed

DIRECTIONS

1. Soak the quinoa and goji grains for 5-6 minutes in water
2. Cook quinoa until soft for 10-15 minutes
3. Roast the cumin seeds in a hot pan and stir in goji berries and sprinkle with parsley

Serves:	**2**
Prep Time:	**10** Minutes
Cook Time:	**20** Minutes
Total Time:	**30** Minutes

INGREDIENTS

- 2 cloves garlic
- 2 sausages
- ¼ onion
- ¼ cup carrot
- 2 cups mushrooms
- 1 tsp coconut oil
- ¼ tablespoon parsley
- 2 cups asparagus

DIRECTIONS

1. Sauté the garlic and onions in coconut oil and add the rest of the ingredients
2. Add the sausages and cook for 5-10 minutes, serve when ready

Serves: *3*
Prep Time: *10*   Minutes

Cook Time: *10*   Minutes

Total Time: *20*   Minutes

INGREDIENTS

- 1 cauliflower heat
- 1 tablespoon salt
- 1 tablespoon pepper
- basil
- 1 tablespoon coconut oil
- 1 tablespoon parsley

DIRECTIONS

1. Grate the cauliflower to rice-grain
2. In a pan melt coconut oil add basil and add cauliflower and cook for 5-10 minutes
3. Cook until ready, remove and serve

Serves: **2**

Prep Time: **10** Minutes

Cook Time: **10** Minutes

Total Time: **20** Minutes

INGREDIENTS

- ¼ cup pumpkin seeds
- ¼ cup apricots
- 1 cup pecans
- ¼ cup almonds
- 1 cup coconut
- ½ cup coconut oil
- ½ cup honey
- 1 tsp cinnamon
- ¼ tsp nutmeg

DIRECTIONS

1. Preheat the oven to 325 F
2. Combine all the ingredients and toss well
3. Spread the mixture on a baking sheet (grease it with coconut oil) and bake for 10-15 minutes
4. When ready remove from oven and stir apricots
5. Let it cool and serve

Serves: **2**

Prep Time: **10** Minutes

Cook Time: **10** Minutes

Total Time: **20** Minutes

INGREDIENTS

- 2 eggs
- zest of ½ orange
- butter
- 2 tablespoons milk
- 10 slices fruit bread

DIRECTIONS

1. In a bowl mix eggs, orange zest and eggs, beat the eggs before and mix everything together
2. Place a slice of bread into the mixture to soak
3. Place a pan over medium heat
4. Place the bread slices in the pan and cook for 1-2 minutes on each side
5. Remove and serve with maple syrup

COCONUT OMELETTE

Serves: **4**

Prep Time: **10** Minutes

Cook Time: **10** Minutes

Total Time: **20** Minutes

INGREDIENTS

- 2 eggs
- ½ tsp honey
- 1 tsp coconut oil

DIRECTIONS

1. In a bowl beat 2 eggs, add honey and stir
2. In a frying pan heat coconut oil over medium heat and pour the mixture
3. Cook on each side for 1-2 minutes
4. Remove and serve with salt or pepper

BANANA BREAKFAST CHEESECAKE

Serves: *1*

Prep Time: *10*   Minutes

Cook Time: *10*   Minutes

Total Time: *20*   Minutes

INGREDIENTS

- 2 tsp chocolate chips
- vanilla extract
- 1 tsp almond butter
- 1 tsp honey
- 2 tablespoons oats
- 1 tablespoon cream cheese
- 1 banana

DIRECTIONS

1. In a bowl mix almond butter, oats and honey
2. Slice a banana and add it to the mixture
3. In the microwave add chocolate chips for 1 minute, add vanilla extract and cream cheese to the melted chocolate
4. Top the banana with chocolate mixture and serve

Serves: **4**

Prep Time: **10**   Minutes

Cook Time: **30**   Minutes

Total Time: **40**   Minutes

INGREDIENTS

- 1 cup whole wheat flour
- ¼ tsp baking soda
- ¼ tsp baking powder
- 2 tablespoons goji berries
- 2 eggs
- 1 cup milk

DIRECTIONS

1. In a bowl combine all ingredients together and mix well
2. In a skillet heat olive oil
3. Pour ¼ of the batter and cook each pancake for 1-2 minutes per side
4. When ready remove from heat and serve

KIWI PANCAKES

Serves: **4**
Prep Time: **10**   Minutes

Cook Time: **20**   Minutes

Total Time: **30**   Minutes

INGREDIENTS

- 1 cup whole wheat flour
- ¼ tsp baking soda
- ¼ tsp baking powder
- 1 cup mashed kiwi
- 2 eggs
- 1 cup milk

DIRECTIONS

1. In a bowl combine all ingredients together and mix well
2. In a skillet heat olive oil
3. Pour ¼ of the batter and cook each pancake for 1-2 minutes per side
4. When ready remove from heat and serve

MANGO PANCAKES

Serves: **4**

Prep Time: **10**   Minutes

Cook Time: **20**   Minutes

Total Time: **30**   Minutes

INGREDIENTS

- 1 cup whole wheat flour
- ¼ tsp baking soda
- ¼ tsp baking powder
- 1 cup mashed mango
- 2 eggs
- 1 cup milk

DIRECTIONS

1. In a bowl combine all ingredients together and mix well
2. In a skillet heat olive oil
3. Pour ¼ of the batter and cook each pancake for 1-2 minutes per side
4. When ready remove from heat and serve

Serves: **4**
Prep Time: **10**   Minutes

Cook Time: **30**   Minutes

Total Time: **40**   Minutes

INGREDIENTS

- 1 cup whole wheat flour
- ¼ tsp baking soda
- ¼ tsp baking powder
- 2 eggs
- 1 cup milk

DIRECTIONS

1. In a bowl combine all ingredients together and mix well
2. In a skillet heat olive oil
3. Pour ¼ of the batter and cook each pancake for 1-2 minutes per side
4. When ready remove from heat and serve

GINGERBREAD MUFFINS

Serves: *8-12*
Prep Time: *10*   Minutes

Cook Time: *20*   Minutes

Total Time: *30*   Minutes

INGREDIENTS

- 2 eggs
- 1 tablespoon olive oil
- 1 cup milk
- 2 cups whole wheat flour
- 1 tsp baking soda
- ¼ tsp baking soda
- 1 tsp ginger
- 1 tsp cinnamon
- ¼ cup molasses

DIRECTIONS

1. In a bowl combine all wet ingredients
2. In another bowl combine all dry ingredients
3. Combine wet and dry ingredients together
4. Fold in ginger and mix well
5. Pour mixture into 8-12 prepared muffin cups, fill 2/3 of the cups

6. Bake for 18-20 minutes at 375 F
7. When ready remove from the oven and serve

PEAR MUFFINS

Serves: *8-12*
Prep Time: *10*   Minutes

Cook Time: *20*   Minutes

Total Time: *30*   Minutes

INGREDIENTS

- 2 eggs
- 1 tablespoon olive oil
- 1 cup milk
- 2 cups whole wheat flour
- 1 tsp baking soda
- ¼ tsp baking soda
- 1 tsp cinnamon
- 1 cup mashed pear

DIRECTIONS

1. In a bowl combine all wet ingredients
2. In another bowl combine all dry ingredients
3. Combine wet and dry ingredients together
4. Pour mixture into 8-12 prepared muffin cups, fill 2/3 of the cups
5. Bake for 18-20 minutes at 375 F
6. When ready remove from the oven and serve

POMELO MUFFINS

Serves: *8-12*
Prep Time: *10*   Minutes

Cook Time: *20*   Minutes

Total Time: *30*   Minutes

INGREDIENTS

- 2 eggs
- 1 tablespoon olive oil
- 1 cup milk
- 2 cups whole wheat flour
- 1 tsp baking soda
- ¼ tsp baking soda
- 1 tsp cinnamon
- 1 cup pomelo

DIRECTIONS

1. In a bowl combine all wet ingredients
2. In another bowl combine all dry ingredients
3. Combine wet and dry ingredients together
4. Pour mixture into 8-12 prepared muffin cups, fill 2/3 of the cups
5. Bake for 18-20 minutes at 375 F
6. When ready remove from the oven and serve

APPLE MUFFINS

Serves: **8-12**

Prep Time: **10** Minutes

Cook Time: **20** Minutes

Total Time: **30** Minutes

INGREDIENTS

- 2 eggs
- 1 tablespoon olive oil
- 1 cup milk
- 2 cups whole wheat flour
- 1 tsp baking soda
- ¼ tsp baking soda
- 1 tsp cinnamon
- 1 cup apple

DIRECTIONS

1. In a bowl combine all wet ingredients
2. In another bowl combine all dry ingredients
3. Combine wet and dry ingredients together
4. Pour mixture into 8-12 prepared muffin cups, fill 2/3 of the cups
5. Bake for 18-20 minutes at 375 F
6. When ready remove from the oven and serve

CHOCOLATE MUFFINS

Serves: *8-12*
Prep Time: *10*   Minutes

Cook Time: *20*   Minutes

Total Time: *30*   Minutes

INGREDIENTS

- 2 eggs
- 1 tablespoon olive oil
- 1 cup milk
- 2 cups whole wheat flour
- 1 tsp baking soda
- ¼ tsp baking soda
- 1 tsp cinnamon
- 1 cup chocolate chips

DIRECTIONS

1. In a bowl combine all wet ingredients
2. In another bowl combine all dry ingredients
3. Combine wet and dry ingredients together
4. Fold in chocolate chips and mix well
5. Pour mixture into 8-12 prepared muffin cups, fill 2/3 of the cups
6. Bake for 18-20 minutes at 375 F, when ready remove and serve

SIMPLE MUFFINS

Serves: *8-12*

Prep Time: *10*   Minutes

Cook Time: *20*   Minutes

Total Time: *30*   Minutes

INGREDIENTS

- 2 eggs
- 1 tablespoon olive oil
- 1 cup milk
- 2 cups whole wheat flour
- 1 tsp baking soda
- ¼ tsp baking soda
- 1 tsp cinnamon

DIRECTIONS

1. In a bowl combine all wet ingredients
2. In another bowl combine all dry ingredients
3. Combine wet and dry ingredients together
4. Pour mixture into 8-12 prepared muffin cups, fill 2/3 of the cups
5. Bake for 18-20 minutes at 375 F
6. When ready remove from the oven and serve

SPINACH OMELETTE

Serves: **1**
Prep Time: **5**   Minutes

Cook Time: **10**   Minutes

Total Time: **15**   Minutes

INGREDIENTS

- 2 eggs
- ¼ tsp salt
- ¼ tsp black pepper
- 1 tablespoon olive oil
- ¼ cup cheese
- ¼ tsp basil
- 1 cup spinach

DIRECTIONS

1. In a bowl combine all ingredients together and mix well
2. In a skillet heat olive oil and pour the egg mixture
3. Cook for 1-2 minutes per side
4. When ready remove omelette from the skillet and serve

CUCUMBER OMELETTE

Serves: **1**

Prep Time: **5** Minutes

Cook Time: **10** Minutes

Total Time: **15** Minutes

INGREDIENTS

- 2 eggs
- ¼ tsp salt
- ¼ tsp black pepper
- 1 tablespoon olive oil
- ¼ cup cheese
- ¼ tsp basil
- ½ cup cucumber

DIRECTIONS

1. In a bowl combine all ingredients together and mix well
2. In a skillet heat olive oil and pour the egg mixture
3. Cook for 1-2 minutes per side
4. When ready remove omelette from the skillet and serve

BASIL OMELETTE

Serves: **1**
Prep Time: **5**   Minutes

Cook Time: **10**   Minutes

Total Time: **15**   Minutes

INGREDIENTS

- 2 eggs
- ¼ tsp salt
- ¼ tsp black pepper
- 1 tablespoon olive oil
- ¼ cup cheese
- ¼ tsp basil
- 1 cup red onion

DIRECTIONS

1. In a bowl combine all ingredients together and mix well
2. In a skillet heat olive oil and pour the egg mixture
3. Cook for 1-2 minutes per side
4. When ready remove omelette from the skillet and serve

CHEESE OMELETTE

Serves: *1*
Prep Time: 5   Minutes

Cook Time: *10*   Minutes

Total Time: *15*   Minutes

INGREDIENTS

- 2 eggs
- ¼ tsp salt
- ¼ tsp black pepper
- 1 tablespoon olive oil
- ¼ cup cheese
- ¼ tsp basil
- 1 cup mushrooms

DIRECTIONS

1. In a bowl combine all ingredients together and mix well
2. In a skillet heat olive oil and pour the egg mixture
3. Cook for 1-2 minutes per side
4. When ready remove omelette from the skillet and serve

OLIVE OMELETTE

Serves: **1**

Prep Time: **5**   Minutes

Cook Time: **10**   Minutes

Total Time: **15**   Minutes

INGREDIENTS

- 2 eggs
- ¼ tsp salt
- ¼ tsp black pepper
- 1 tablespoon olive oil
- ¼ cup cheese
- ¼ cup Kalamata olives
- ¼ tsp basil
- 1 cup tomatoes

DIRECTIONS

1. In a bowl combine all ingredients together and mix well
2. In a skillet heat olive oil and pour the egg mixture
3. Cook for 1-2 minutes per side
4. When ready remove omelette from the skillet and serve

CARDAMOM TART

Serves: *6-8*

Prep Time: **25**   Minutes

Cook Time: **25**   Minutes

Total Time: *50*   Minutes

INGREDIENTS

- 4-5 pears
- 2 tablespoons lemon juice
- pastry sheets

CARDAMOM FILLING

- ½ lb. butter
- ½ lb. brown sugar
- ½ lb. almonds
- ¼ lb. flour
- 1 ¼ tsp cardamom
- 2 eggs

DIRECTIONS

1. Preheat oven to 400 F, unfold pastry sheets and place them on a baking sheet
2. Toss together all ingredients together and mix well

3. Spread mixture in a single layer on the pastry sheets
4. Before baking decorate with your desired fruits
5. Bake at 400 F for 22-25 minutes or until golden brown
6. When ready remove from the oven and serve

APPLE TART

Serves: *6-8*
Prep Time: **25** Minutes

Cook Time: **25** Minutes

Total Time: **50** Minutes

INGREDIENTS

- pastry sheets

FILLING

- 1 tsp lemon juice
- 3 oz. brown sugar
- 1 lb. apples
- 150 ml double cream
- 2 eggs

DIRECTIONS

1. Preheat oven to 400 F, unfold pastry sheets and place them on a baking sheet
2. Toss together all ingredients together and mix well
3. Spread mixture in a single layer on the pastry sheets
4. Before baking decorate with your desired fruits
5. Bake at 400 F for 22-25 minutes or until golden brown
6. When ready remove from the oven and serve

PIE RECIPES

PEACH PECAN PIE

Serves: **8-12**

Prep Time: **15**   Minutes
Cook Time: **35**   Minutes
Total Time: **50**   Minutes

INGREDIENTS

- 4-5 cups peaches
- 1 tablespoon preserves
- 1 cup sugar
- 4 small egg yolks
- ¼ cup flour
- 1 tsp vanilla extract

DIRECTIONS

1. Line a pie plate or pie form with pastry and cover the edges of the plate depending on your preference
2. In a bowl combine all pie ingredients together and mix well
3. Pour the mixture over the pastry
4. Bake at 400-425 F for 25-30 minutes or until golden brown
5. When ready remove from the oven and let it rest for 15 minutes

GRAPEFRUIT PIE

Serves: *8-12*

Prep Time: *15*   Minutes

Cook Time: *35*   Minutes

Total Time: *50*   Minutes

INGREDIENTS

- pastry sheets
- 2 cups grapefruit
- 1 cup brown sugar
- ¼ cup flour
- 5-6 egg yolks
- 5 oz. butter

DIRECTIONS

1. Line a pie plate or pie form with pastry and cover the edges of the plate depending on your preference
2. In a bowl combine all pie ingredients together and mix well
3. Pour the mixture over the pastry
4. Bake at 400-425 F for 25-30 minutes or until golden brown
5. When ready remove from the oven and let it rest for 15 minutes

BUTTERFINGER PIE

Serves: **8-12**

Prep Time: **15** Minutes

Cook Time: **35** Minutes

Total Time: **50** Minutes

INGREDIENTS

- pastry sheets
- 1 package cream cheese
- 1 tsp vanilla extract
- ¼ cup peanut butter
- 1 cup powdered sugar (to decorate)
- 2 cups Butterfinger candy bars
- 8 oz whipped topping

DIRECTIONS

1. Line a pie plate or pie form with pastry and cover the edges of the plate depending on your preference
2. In a bowl combine all pie ingredients together and mix well
3. Pour the mixture over the pastry
4. Bake at 400-425 F for 25-30 minutes or until golden brown
5. When ready remove from the oven and let it rest for 15 minutes

SMOOTHIE RECIPES

BANANA MATCHA SMOOTHIE

Serves: **1**
Prep Time: **5**   Minutes

Cook Time: **5**   Minutes

Total Time: **10** Minutes

INGREDIENTS

- 1 cup banana
- 1 tsp matcha powder
- 1 cup spinach
- 1 tsp flax seed
- 1 tsp vanilla extract
- 1 cup soy milk

DIRECTIONS

1. In a blender place all ingredients and blend until smooth
2. Pour smoothie in a glass and serve

PROTEIN SMOOTHIE

Serves: **1**
Prep Time: **5**   Minutes

Cook Time: **5**   Minutes

Total Time: **10**   Minutes

INGREDIENTS

- 2 bananas
- 2 dates
- 1 cup kale
- 1 cup spinach
- 2 tablespoons cocoa powder
- 1 tsp vanilla extract
- 1 cup nut milk

DIRECTIONS

1. In a blender place all ingredients and blend until smooth
2. Pour smoothie in a glass and serve

Serves: *1*
Prep Time: 5   Minutes

Cook Time: 5   Minutes

Total Time: *10*   Minutes

INGREDIENTS

- 1 cup strawberries
- 1 banana
- 1 cup Greek Yogurt
- 1 cup soy milk
- 1 tsp vanilla extract
- 1 tsp chia seeds

DIRECTIONS

1. In a blender place all ingredients and blend until smooth
2. Pour smoothie in a glass and serve

Serves: *1*
Prep Time: *5*   Minutes

Cook Time: *5*   Minutes

Total Time: *10*   Minutes

INGREDIENTS

- 1 cup strawberries
- 1 banana
- 1 cup Greek Yogurt
- 1 scoop protein powder
- 1 tsp hemp seeds
- ½ cup chocolate chips

DIRECTIONS

1. In a blender place all ingredients and blend until smooth
2. Pour smoothie in a glass and serve

APPLE SMOOTHIE

Serves: **1**

Prep Time: **5**   Minutes

Cook Time: **5**   Minutes

Total Time: **10**   Minutes

INGREDIENTS

- 1 apple
- 2 pears
- ½ cup rolled oats
- 1 tsp cinnamon
- 1 cup nut milk

DIRECTIONS

1. In a blender place all ingredients and blend until smooth
2. Pour smoothie in a glass and serve

SPINACH SMOOTHIE

Serves: **1**

Prep Time: **5**   Minutes

Cook Time: **5**   Minutes

Total Time: **10**   Minutes

INGREDIENTS

- 1 banana
- 1 cup vanilla yogurt
- 1 cup spinach
- 1 cup kale
- 1 cup orange juice

DIRECTIONS

1. In a blender place all ingredients and blend until smooth
2. Pour smoothie in a glass and serve

PEANUT BUTTER SMOOTHIE

Serves: *1*
Prep Time: 5   Minutes

Cook Time: 5   Minutes

Total Time: *10*   Minutes

INGREDIENTS

- 1 cup berries
- 2 tablespoons peanut butter
- ½ cup protein powder
- ½ cup oats
- 1 cup soy milk

DIRECTIONS

1. In a blender place all ingredients and blend until smooth
2. Pour smoothie in a glass and serve

PINEAPPLE SMOOTHIE

Serves: **1**

Prep Time: **5** Minutes

Cook Time: **5** Minutes

Total Time: **10** Minutes

INGREDIENTS

- 1 cup pineapple
- 1 cup strawberries
- 1 cup Greek yogurt
- 1 cup soy milk
- 1 cup ice

DIRECTIONS

1. In a blender place all ingredients and blend until smooth
2. Pour smoothie in a glass and serve

ORANGE SMOOTHIE

Serves: *1*

Prep Time: 5   Minutes

Cook Time: 5   Minutes

Total Time: *10*   Minutes

INGREDIENTS

- 1 orange
- ½ cup orange juice
- ½ banana
- 1 tsp vanilla essence

DIRECTIONS

1. In a blender place all ingredients and blend until smooth
2. Pour smoothie in a glass and serve

RAISIN DATE SMOOTHIE

Serves: **1**

Prep Time: **5**   Minutes

Cook Time: **5**   Minutes

Total Time: **10**   Minutes

INGREDIENTS

- ¼ cup raisins
- 2 Medjool dates
- 1 cup berries
- 1 cup almond milk
- 1 tsp chia seeds

DIRECTIONS

1. In a blender place all ingredients and blend until smooth
2. Pour smoothie in a glass and serve

ICE-CREAM RECIPES

PISTACHIOS ICE-CREAM

Serves: **6-8**

Prep Time: **15**   Minutes

Cook Time: **15**   Minutes

Total Time: **30**   Minutes

INGREDIENTS

- 4 egg yolks
- 1 cup heavy cream
- 1 cup milk
- 1 cup sugar
- 1 vanilla bean
- 1 tsp almond extract
- 1 cup cherries
- ½ cup pistachios

DIRECTIONS

1. In a saucepan whisk together all ingredients
2. Mix until bubbly
3. Strain into a bowl and cool
4. Whisk in favorite fruits and mix well
5. Cover and refrigerate for 2-3 hours

6. Pour mixture in the ice-cream maker and follow manufacturer instructions
7. Serve when ready

VANILLA ICE-CREAM

Serves: *6-8*

Prep Time: *15*   Minutes
Cook Time: *15*   Minutes
Total Time: *30*   Minutes

INGREDIENTS

- 1 cup milk
- 1 tablespoon cornstarch
- 1 oz. cream cheese
- 1 cup heavy cream
- 1 cup brown sugar
- 1 tablespoon corn syrup
- 1 vanilla bean

DIRECTIONS

1. In a saucepan whisk together all ingredients
2. Mix until bubbly
3. Strain into a bowl and cool
4. Whisk in favorite fruits and mix well
5. Cover and refrigerate for 2-3 hours
6. Pour mixture in the ice-cream maker and follow manufacturer instructions
7. Serve when ready

Serves: *6-8*

Prep Time: *15*   Minutes

Cook Time: *15*   Minutes

Total Time: *30*   Minutes

INGREDIENTS

- 4 egg yolks
- 1 cup black coffee
- 2 cups heavy cream
- 1 cup half-and-half
- 1 cup brown sugar
- 1 tsp vanilla extract

DIRECTIONS

1. In a saucepan whisk together all ingredients
2. Mix until bubbly
3. Strain into a bowl and cool
4. Whisk in favorite fruits and mix well
5. Cover and refrigerate for 2-3 hours
6. Pour mixture in the ice-cream maker and follow manufacturer instructions
7. Serve when ready

FOURTH COOKBOOK

CHICKEN PIZZA

Serves: **2**

Prep Time: **10** Minutes

Cook Time: **20** Minutes

Total Time: **30** Minutes

INGREDIENTS

- 1 ready-made pizza crust
- 1 tsp olive oil
- 1 cup onion
- 14 cup red pepper strips
- 1 cup chicken
- ¼ cup barbecue sauce
- 1 cup mozzarella cheese
- topping of any choice

DIRECTIONS

1. Preheat the oven to 425 F
2. In a frying pan add pepper strips, onion, chicken and cook on low heat
3. Cook until ready and remove from heat

4. Place crust on a cookie sheet and spread barbecue sauce, and the rest of ingredients on the crust

5. Top with mozzarella and bake for 12-15 minutes

6. Remove and serve

CIABATTA PIZZA

Serves: **2**

Prep Time: **10** Minutes

Cook Time: **20** Minutes

Total Time: **30** Minutes

INGREDIENTS

- 1 loaf ciabatta
- 1 cup tomato sauce
- 1 zucchini
- ½ cup mushrooms
- 1 cup mozzarella cheese
- 1 tablespoon basil

DIRECTIONS

1. Preheat the oven to 375 F
2. Cum ciabatta lengthwise and place on a cookie sheet
3. Spread sauce, zucchini, mushrooms on each one and top with mozzarella
4. Sprinkle basil, bake for 12-15 minutes, remove and serve

FIESTA SHRIMP

Serves: **2**

Prep Time: **10**   Minutes

Cook Time: **10**   Minutes

Total Time: **20**   Minutes

INGREDIENTS

- 3 oz. shrimp
- ½ cup zucchini
- ½ cup fiesta garden salsa
- ½ oz. Monterey Jack cheese
- cilantro
- 1 tortilla

DIRECTIONS

1. In a bowl add zucchini, shrimp and salsa
2. Microwave for 4-5 minutes, remove and add grated cheese
3. Sprinkle cilantro and pour mixture over tortilla
4. Serve when ready

Serves: *2*
Prep Time: *10*   Minutes

Cook Time: *10*   Minutes

Total Time: *20*   Minutes

INGREDIENTS

- 2 salmon steaks
- 1 tablespoon dipping sauce
- 1 tsp cooking oil

DIRECTIONS

1. Preheat grill
2. Baste salmon steaks with sauce and cook for 5-6 minutes
3. Remove and serve

ORIENTAL GREENS

Serves: **2**

Prep Time: **10** Minutes

Cook Time: **10** Minutes

Total Time: **20** Minutes

INGREDIENTS

- ½ cup green beans
- ¼ cup snow peas
- 1 cup cauliflower florets
- 1 cup water chestnuts
- 2 radishes
- 2 scallions
- ½ cup red onion
- 1 tsp powdered ginger
- ½ cup rice wine vinegar

DIRECTIONS

1. In a bowl mix cauliflower floret, onions, chestnuts, radish, beans and snow peas
2. In another bowl mix rice wine vinegar, ginger, pour over vegetables and mix well
3. Mix well and serv

SHRIMP PIZZA

Serves: 2

Prep Time: *10*   Minutes

Cook Time: *20*   Minutes

Total Time: *30*   Minutes

INGREDIENTS

- 13 oz. pizza dough
- 1 tablespoon cornmeal
- ¼ cup ricotta cheese
- 1 lb. shrimp
- 5 cloves garlic
- 1 cup mozzarella cheese
- 1 tablespoon dried basil

DIRECTIONS

1. Preheat the oven to 375 F
2. In a baking pan sprinkle cornmeal and add the pizza dough, bake for 6-8 minutes
3. Remove and cover pizza with mozzarella, ricotta, garlic and sprinkle with basil
4. Bake for 12-15 minutes, remove and serve

COLE SLAW

Serves: **2**

Prep Time: **10**   Minutes

Cook Time: **10**   Minutes

Total Time: **20**   Minutes

INGREDIENTS

- 1/3 cup vinegar
- ¼ cup whipping cream
- 2 eggs
- ½ cup Splenda
- pinch of salt
- 1 tablespoon butter
- 1 lb. cabbage

DIRECTIONS

1. In a saucepan add vinegar, whipping cream, eggs, Splenda, and salt and cook for 10-12 minutes
2. Add butter, cabbage, toss to coat and mix well
3. Remove from heat add, walnuts and serve

DIJON VINAIGRETTE

Serves: **2**
Prep Time: **5**   Minutes

Cook Time: **5**   Minutes

Total Time: **10** Minutes

INGREDIENTS

- 2 tablespoons red wine vinegar
- 1 tablespoon water
- 1 tablespoon olive oil
- 1 tsp Dijon mustard
- ½ tsp garlic powder

DIRECTIONS

1. In a bowl mix all ingredients
2. Chill overnight and serve

COTTAGE CHEESE CASSEROLE

Serves: **3**

Prep Time: **10**   Minutes

Cook Time: **50**   Minutes

Total Time: **60**   Minutes

INGREDIENTS

- 2 eggs
- 2 cups cottage cheese
- 1 red onion
- 1 pinch of pepper

DIRECTIONS

1. In a bowl mix all ingredients and pour into a casserole dish
2. Bake at 325 for 50 minutes
3. Remove and serve

FRENCH DRESSING

Serves: **2**
Prep Time: **5**   Minutes

Cook Time: **5**   Minutes

Total Time: **10**   Minutes

INGREDIENTS

- ½ cup ketchup
- ¼ cup oil
- ¼ cup white vinegar
- 1 tsp lemon juice
- dash of pepper

DIRECTIONS

1. In a bowl mix all ingredients
2. Chill overnight and serve

TAPENADE

Serves: **4**

Prep Time: **10**   Minutes

Cook Time: **10**   Minutes

Total Time: **20**   Minutes

INGREDIENTS

- ½ cup Kalamata olives
- 1 tsp capers
- ½ cup olive oil
- 1 tablespoon balsamic vinegar

DIRECTIONS

1. In a bowl chop olive and mix with crushed garlic
2. Add the rest of ingredients and mix well
3. Chill for 1-2 hours serve with asparagus or vegetables

Serves: **2**

Prep Time: **10**   Minutes

Cook Time: **20**   Minutes

Total Time: **30**   Minutes

INGREDIENTS

- ½ lb. asparagus
- 1 tablespoon olive oil
- ½ red onion
- 2 eggs
- ¼ tsp salt
- 2 oz. cheddar cheese
- 1 garlic clove
- ¼ tsp dill

DIRECTIONS

1. In a bowl whisk eggs with salt and cheese
2. In a frying pan heat olive oil and pour egg mixture
3. Add remaining ingredients and mix well
4. Serve when ready

Serves: **2**
Prep Time: **10** Minutes

Cook Time: **20** Minutes

Total Time: **30** Minutes

INGREDIENTS

- 1 tablespoon olive oil
- ½ red onion
- 2 eggs
- ¼ tsp salt
- 2 oz. cheddar cheese
- 1 garlic clove
- ¼ tsp dill
- 1 cup tomato

DIRECTIONS

1. In a bowl whisk eggs with salt and cheese
2. In a frying pan heat olive oil and pour egg mixture
3. Add remaining ingredients and mix well
4. Serve when ready

KALE FRITATTA

Serves: 2

Prep Time: 10   Minutes

Cook Time: 20   Minutes

Total Time: 30   Minutes

INGREDIENTS

- 1 cup kale
- 1 tablespoon olive oil
- ½ red onion
- 2 eggs
- ¼ tsp salt
- 2 oz. cheddar cheese
- 1 garlic clove
- ¼ tsp dill

DIRECTIONS

1. In a bowl whisk eggs with salt and cheese
2. In a frying pan heat olive oil and pour egg mixture
3. Add remaining ingredients and mix well
4. Serve when ready

Serves: **2**
Prep Time: **10**   Minutes

Cook Time: **20**   Minutes

Total Time: **30**   Minutes

INGREDIENTS

- 1 cup turnip
- 2 eggs
- 1 tablespoon olive oil
- ½ red onion
- ¼ tsp salt
- 2 oz. parmesan cheese
- 1 garlic clove
- ¼ tsp dill

DIRECTIONS

1. In a bowl whisk eggs with salt and cheese
2. In a frying pan heat olive oil and pour egg mixture
3. Add remaining ingredients and mix well
4. Serve when ready

SWISS CHARD FRITATTA

Serves: **2**

Prep Time: **10** Minutes

Cook Time: **20** Minutes

Total Time: **30** Minutes

INGREDIENTS

- 1 tablespoon olive oil
- ½ red onion
- ¼ cup swiss chard
- ¼ tsp salt
- 2 oz. cheddar cheese
- 1 garlic clove
- ¼ tsp dill

DIRECTIONS

1. In a bowl whisk eggs with salt and cheese
2. In a frying pan heat olive oil and pour egg mixture
3. Add remaining ingredients and mix well
4. Serve when ready

AVOCADO SANDWICH

Serves: *1*

Prep Time: *5* Minutes

Cook Time: *15* Minutes

Total Time: *20* Minutes

INGREDIENTS

- 2 slices bread
- 1 cup hummus
- 1 cup sauerkraut
- 1 avocado

DIRECTIONS

1. Spread sauerkraut, avocado and hummus in each bread slice
2. Place the sandwich in a baking dish and bake at 325 F for 5-6 minutes
3. When crispy remove from the oven and serve

Serves: **4**

Prep Time: **10** Minutes

Cook Time: **30** Minutes

Total Time: **40** Minutes

INGREDIENTS

- 1 carrot
- ¼ cucumber
- ¼ cup shallots
- ¼ cup jalapeno
- 1 tablespoon sugar
- 1 tablespoon fish sauce
- 1 cup tomatoes
- 10 oz. smoked trout fillets
- ¼ cup basil leaves
- ¼ cup chili sauce
- ¼ cup roasted peanuts
- lettuce leaves

DIRECTIONS

1. In a bowl add shallots, fish sauce, sugar and mix well
2. Add the trout fillets and tomatoes to the marinade and toss well
3. Arrange lettuce leaves on a plate and place the trout fillets with the remaining ingredients
4. Serve when ready

Serves: **2**

Prep Time: **5** Minutes

Cook Time: **15** Minutes

Total Time: **20** Minutes

INGREDIENTS

- 2 tablespoons olive oil
- 1 onion
- 1 cup almond milk
- 1 tsp curry powder
- 1 lb. shrimp
- 1 cup cauliflower

DIRECTIONS

1. In a skillet heat olive oil and sauté onion and cauliflower until soft
2. Add almond milk, curry powder, shrimp and cook until shrimp is cooked
3. When ready remove from the skillet and serve

SALMON CROQUETTES

Serves: **4-6**
Prep Time: **10**   Minutes

Cook Time: **20**   Minutes

Total Time: **30**   Minutes

INGREDIENTS

- 1 tin salmon
- 1 onion
- 1 lb. polenta
- ½ lb. flour
- 1 cup olive oil
- 1 green pepper
- 1 tsp salt

DIRECTIONS

1. In a bowl combine green peppers, onion and salmon
2. Season with salt and roll salmon into a bowl with polenta and flour
3. Place the salmon patties in a frying pan and fry until golden brown
4. When ready remove from the pan and serve

SALMON FISH CAKES

Serves: **4-6**

Prep Time: **10** Minutes

Cook Time: **20** Minutes

Total Time: **30** Minutes

INGREDIENTS

- ½ lb. salmon fillets
- 1 lb. mashed potato
- 1 handful of parsley
- ¼ lb. peas
- 1 tablespoon olive oil

DIRECTIONS

1. In a frying pan fry salmon fillets until golden brown
2. Mash the potato, add peas and parsley and mix well
3. Add salmon to the mashed potato mixture and mix everything together
4. Form patties and fry each one for 2-3 minutes
5. When ready remove from skillet

Serves: *3-4*
Prep Time: *10*   Minutes

Cook Time: *20*   Minutes

Total Time: *30*   Minutes

INGREDIENTS

- 2 delicata squashes
- 2 tablespoons olive oil
- 1 tsp curry powder
- 1 tsp salt

DIRECTIONS

1. Preheat the oven to 400 F
2. Cut everything in half lengthwise
3. Toss everything with olive oil and place onto a prepared baking sheet
4. Roast for 18-20 minutes at 400 F or until golden brown
5. When ready remove from the oven and serve

Serves: *2*

Prep Time: *10*   Minutes

Cook Time: *20*   Minutes

Total Time: *30*   Minutes

INGREDIENTS

- 1 lb. brussels sprouts
- 1 tablespoon olive oil
- 1 tablespoon parmesan cheese
- 1 tsp garlic powder
- 1 tsp seasoning

DIRECTIONS

1. Preheat the oven to 425 F
2. In a bowl toss everything with olive oil and seasoning
3. Spread everything onto a prepared baking sheet
4. Bake for 8-10 minutes or until crisp
5. When ready remove from the oven and serve

CARROT CHIPS

Serves: *2*

Prep Time: *10*   Minutes

Cook Time: *20*   Minutes

Total Time: *30*   Minutes

INGREDIENTS

- 1 lb. carrot
- 1 tablespoon olive oil
- 1 tablespoon parmesan cheese
- 1 tsp garlic powder
- 1 tsp seasoning

DIRECTIONS

1. Preheat the oven to 425 F
2. In a bowl toss everything with olive oil and seasoning
3. Spread everything onto a prepared baking sheet
4. Bake for 8-10 minutes or until crisp
5. When ready remove from the oven and serve

Serves: 2

Prep Time: 10   Minutes

Cook Time: 20   Minutes

Total Time: 30   Minutes

INGREDIENTS

- 1 lb. beet
- 1 tablespoon olive oil
- 1 tablespoon parmesan cheese
- 1 tsp garlic powder
- 1 tsp seasoning

DIRECTIONS

1. Preheat the oven to 425 F
2. In a bowl toss everything with olive oil and seasoning
3. Spread everything onto a prepared baking sheet
4. Bake for 8-10 minutes or until crisp
5. When ready remove from the oven and serve

Serves: **2**
Prep Time: **10** Minutes

Cook Time: **20** Minutes

Total Time: **30** Minutes

INGREDIENTS

- 1 lb. parsnip
- 1 tablespoon olive oil
- 1 tablespoon parmesan cheese
- 1 tsp garlic powder
- 1 tsp seasoning

DIRECTIONS

1. Preheat the oven to 425 F
2. In a bowl toss everything with olive oil and seasoning
3. Spread everything onto a prepared baking sheet
4. Bake for 8-10 minutes or until crisp
5. When ready remove from the oven and serve

Serves: **2**

Prep Time: **10** Minutes

Cook Time: **20** Minutes

Total Time: **30** Minutes

INGREDIENTS

- 1 lb. radish
- 1 tablespoon olive oil
- 1 tablespoon parmesan cheese
- 1 tsp garlic powder
- 1 tsp seasoning

DIRECTIONS

1. Preheat the oven to 425 F
2. In a bowl toss everything with olive oil and seasoning
3. Spread everything onto a prepared baking sheet
4. Bake for 8-10 minutes or until crisp
5. When ready remove from the oven and serve

Serves: **2**

Prep Time: **10** Minutes

Cook Time: **20** Minutes

Total Time: **30** Minutes

INGREDIENTS

- 1 lb. taro
- 1 tablespoon olive oil
- 1 tablespoon parmesan cheese
- 1 tsp garlic powder
- 1 tsp seasoning

DIRECTIONS

1. Preheat the oven to 425 F
2. In a bowl toss everything with olive oil and seasoning
3. Spread everything onto a prepared baking sheet
4. Bake for 8-10 minutes or until crisp
5. When ready remove from the oven and serve

Serves: *2*
Prep Time: *10*   Minutes

Cook Time: *20*   Minutes

Total Time: *30*   Minutes

INGREDIENTS

- ½ lb. garlic
- 1 tablespoon olive oil
- 1 tablespoon parmesan cheese
- 1 tsp garlic powder
- 1 tsp seasoning

DIRECTIONS

1. Preheat the oven to 425 F
2. In a bowl toss everything with olive oil and seasoning
3. Spread everything onto a prepared baking sheet
4. Bake for 8-10 minutes or until crisp
5. When ready remove from the oven and serve

SPINACH CHIPS

Serves: 2

Prep Time: *10* Minutes

Cook Time: *20* Minutes

Total Time: *30* Minutes

INGREDIENTS

- 1 lb. spinach
- 1 tablespoon olive oil
- 1 tablespoon parmesan cheese
- 1 tsp garlic powder
- 1 tsp seasoning

DIRECTIONS

1. Preheat the oven to 425 F
2. In a bowl toss everything with olive oil and seasoning
3. Spread everything onto a prepared baking sheet
4. Bake for 8-10 minutes or until crisp
5. When ready remove from the oven and serve

PASTA

SIMPLE SPAGHETTI

Serves: 2

Prep Time: 5   Minutes

Cook Time: 15   Minutes

Total Time: 20   Minutes

INGREDIENTS

- 10 oz. spaghetti
- 2 eggs
- ½ cup parmesan cheese
- 1 tsp black pepper
- Olive oil
- 1 tsp parsley
- 2 cloves garlic

DIRECTIONS

1. In a pot boil spaghetti (or any other type of pasta), drain and set aside
2. In a bowl whish eggs with parmesan cheese
3. In a skillet heat olive oil, add garlic and cook for 1-2 minutes
4. Pour egg mixture and mix well
5. Add pasta and stir well

6. When ready garnish with parsley and serve

PASTA WITH OLIVES AND TOMATOES

Serves: **2**

Prep Time: **5** Minutes

Cook Time: **15** Minutes

Total Time: **20** Minutes

INGREDIENTS

- 8 oz. pasta
- 3 tablespoons olive oil
- 2 cloves garlic
- 5-6 anchovy fillets
- 2 cups tomatoes
- 1 cup olives
- ½ cup basil leaves

DIRECTIONS

1. In a pot boil spaghetti (or any other type of pasta), drain and set aside
2. Place all the ingredients for the sauce in a pot and bring to a simmer
3. Add pasta and mix well
4. When ready garnish with parmesan cheese and serve

SALAD

CHICKEN SALAD

Serves: *1*

Prep Time: *5*   Minutes

Cook Time: *5*   Minutes

Total Time: *10* Minutes

INGREDIENTS

- 2 cups cooked chicken breast
- 1 cup mayonnaise
- 1 tsp paprika
- 1 cup celery
- 1 green onion
- ¼ cup green bell pepper
- 1 cup pecans

DIRECTIONS

1. In a bowl mix all ingredients and mix well
2. Serve with dressing

Serves: *1*

Prep Time: 5   Minutes

Cook Time: 5   Minutes

Total Time: *10* Minutes

INGREDIENTS

- 1 egg
- 1 can tuna
- 2 tablespoons mayonnaise
- 2 stalks celery
- Pinch of salt

DIRECTIONS

1. In a bowl combin all ingredients together and mix well
2. Serve with dressing

Serves: *1*
Prep Time: 5   Minutes

Cook Time: 5   Minutes

Total Time: *10*   Minutes

INGREDIENTS

- ¼ cup apple cider vinegar
- ¼ cup vegetable oil
- ¼ tsp paprika
- ¼ cup almonds
- 1-quart strawberries
- 1 romaine lettuce

DIRECTIONS

1. In a bowl combin all ingredients together and mix well
2. Serve with dressing

Serves: *1*

Prep Time: 5   Minutes

Cook Time: 5   Minutes

Total Time: *10*   Minutes

INGREDIENTS

- 4 beets
- 2 tablespoons balsamic vinegar
- 1 tsp maple syrup
- ¼ cup tomatoes
- ¼ cup cucumber

DIRECTIONS

1. In a bowl combin all ingredients together and mix well
2. Serve with dressing

TACO SLAW

Serves: **1**

Prep Time: **5** Minutes

Cook Time: **5** Minutes

Total Time: **10** Minutes

INGREDIENTS

- ½ cabbage
- ¼ red onion
- 1 carrot
- 1 tablespoon cilantro
- ¼ lemon

DIRECTIONS

1. In a bowl combin all ingredients together and mix well
2. Serve with dressing

Serves: **1**
Prep Time: **5**   Minutes

Cook Time: **5**   Minutes

Total Time: **10** Minutes

INGREDIENTS

- 1 package fusilli pasta
- 2 cups tomatoes
- ¼ cup cheese
- ¼ lb. salami
- 1 green bell pepper
- 1 can black olives
- 1 can salad dressing

DIRECTIONS

1. In a bowl combin all ingredients together and mix well
2. Serve with dressing

Serves: *1*

Prep Time: 5   Minutes

Cook Time: 5   Minutes

Total Time: *10*   Minutes

INGREDIENTS

- 2 cucumber
- 1 cup feta cheese
- 1 cup olive
- ¼ cup red onion
- 1 tablespoon olive oil

DIRECTIONS

1. In a bowl combin all ingredients together and mix well
2. Serve with dressing

Serves: **1**

Prep Time: **5**   Minutes

Cook Time: **5**   Minutes

Total Time: **10**   Minutes

INGREDIENTS

- ¼ cup almonds
- 1 lb. spinach
- 1 cup cranberries
- 1 tablespoon sesame seeds
- ¼ tsp paprika
- ¼ cup apple cider vinegar

DIRECTIONS

1. In a bowl combin all ingredients together and mix well
2. Serve with dressing

BEAN SALAD

Serves: *1*

Prep Time: 5   Minutes

Cook Time: 5   Minutes

Total Time: *10*   Minutes

INGREDIENTS

- 10 oz. black beans
- 10 oz. corn kernels
- 10 oz. kidney beans
- 1 green bell pepper
- 1 red bell pepper
- 1 red onion
- ¼ cup olive oil
- 1 tablespoon lime juice
- ¼ tsp chili powder

DIRECTIONS

1. In a bowl combin all ingredients together and mix well
2. Serve with dressing

FIFTH COOKBOOK

BANANA PANCAKES

Serves: **4**

Prep Time: **10** Minutes

Cook Time: **20** Minutes

Total Time: **30** Minutes

INGREDIENTS

- 1 cup whole wheat flour
- ¼ tsp baking soda
- ¼ tsp baking powder
- 1 cup banana
- 2 eggs
- 1 cup milk

DIRECTIONS

5. In a bowl combine all ingredients together and mix well
6. In a skillet heat olive oil
7. Pour ¼ of the batter and cook each pancake for 1-2 minutes per side
8. When ready remove from heat and serve

ALMOND PANCAKES

Serves: **4**
Prep Time: **10** Minutes

Cook Time: **30** Minutes

Total Time: **40** Minutes

INGREDIENTS

- 1 cup whole wheat flour
- ¼ tsp baking soda
- ¼ tsp baking powder
- 1 cup almonds
- 2 eggs
- 1 cup milk

DIRECTIONS

1. In a bowl combine all ingredients together and mix well
2. In a skillet heat olive oil
3. Pour ¼ of the batter and cook each pancake for 1-2 minutes per side
4. When ready remove from heat and serve

Serves: **4**

Prep Time: **10**   Minutes

Cook Time: **20**   Minutes

Total Time: **30**   Minutes

INGREDIENTS

- 1 cup whole wheat flour
- ¼ tsp baking soda
- ¼ tsp baking powder
- 1 cup mashed apricots
- 2 eggs
- 1 cup milk

DIRECTIONS

1. In a bowl combine all ingredients together and mix well
2. In a skillet heat olive oil
3. Pour ¼ of the batter and cook each pancake for 1-2 minutes per side
4. When ready remove from heat and serve

Serves: **4**

Prep Time: **10** Minutes

Cook Time: **20** Minutes

Total Time: **30** Minutes

INGREDIENTS

- 1 cup whole wheat flour
- ¼ tsp baking soda
- ¼ tsp baking powder
- 1 cup strawberries
- 2 eggs
- 1 cup milk

DIRECTIONS

1. In a bowl combine all ingredients together and mix well
2. In a skillet heat olive oil
3. Pour ¼ of the batter and cook each pancake for 1-2 minutes per side
4. When ready remove from heat and serve

BLACKBERRIES PANCAKES

Serves: *4*

Prep Time: *10*   Minutes

Cook Time: *30*   Minutes

Total Time: *40*   Minutes

INGREDIENTS

- 1 cup whole wheat flour
- ¼ tsp baking soda
- ¼ tsp baking powder
- 2 eggs
- 1 cup milk
- 1 cup blackberries

DIRECTIONS

1. In a bowl combine all ingredients together and mix well
2. In a skillet heat olive oil
3. Pour ¼ of the batter and cook each pancake for 1-2 minutes per side
4. When ready remove from heat and serve

Serves: **8-12**

Prep Time: **10** Minutes

Cook Time: **20** Minutes

Total Time: **30** Minutes

INGREDIENTS

- 2 eggs
- 1 tablespoon olive oil
- 1 cup milk
- 2 cups whole wheat flour
- 1 tsp baking soda
- ¼ tsp baking soda
- 1 tsp ginger
- 1 tsp cinnamon
- ¼ cup molasses

DIRECTIONS

1. In a bowl combine all wet ingredients
2. In another bowl combine all dry ingredients
3. Combine wet and dry ingredients together
4. Fold in ginger and mix well
5. Pour mixture into 8-12 prepared muffin cups, fill 2/3 of the cups

222

6. Bake for 18-20 minutes at 375 F
7. When ready remove from the oven and serve

DATE MUFFINS

Serves: *8-12*

Prep Time: *10*   Minutes

Cook Time: *20*   Minutes

Total Time: *30*   Minutes

INGREDIENTS

- 2 eggs
- 1 tablespoon olive oil
- 1 cup milk
- 2 cups whole wheat flour
- 1 tsp baking soda
- ¼ tsp baking soda
- 1 tsp cinnamon
- ½ cup dates

DIRECTIONS

1. In a bowl combine all wet ingredients
2. In another bowl combine all dry ingredients
3. Combine wet and dry ingredients together
4. Pour mixture into 8-12 prepared muffin cups, fill 2/3 of the cups
5. Bake for 18-20 minutes at 375 F
6. When ready remove from the oven and serve

BLUEBERRY MUFFINS

Serves: **8-12**
Prep Time: **10**   Minutes

Cook Time: **20**   Minutes

Total Time: **30**   Minutes

INGREDIENTS

- 2 eggs
- 1 tablespoon olive oil
- 1 cup milk
- 2 cups whole wheat flour
- 1 tsp baking soda
- ¼ tsp baking soda
- 1 tsp cinnamon
- 1 cup blueberries

DIRECTIONS

1. In a bowl combine all wet ingredients
2. In another bowl combine all dry ingredients
3. Combine wet and dry ingredients together
4. Fold in blueberries and mix well
5. Pour mixture into 8-12 prepared muffin cups, fill 2/3 of the cups
6. Bake for 18-20 minutes at 375F

CANTALOUPE MUFFINS

Serves: *8-12*
Prep Time: *10*   Minutes

Cook Time: *20*   Minutes

Total Time: *30*   Minutes

INGREDIENTS

- 2 eggs
- 1 tablespoon olive oil
- 1 cup milk
- 2 cups whole wheat flour
- 1 tsp baking soda
- ¼ tsp baking soda
- 1 tsp cinnamon
- 1 cup cantaloupe

DIRECTIONS

1. In a bowl combine all wet ingredients
2. In another bowl combine all dry ingredients
3. Combine wet and dry ingredients together
4. Pour mixture into 8-12 prepared muffin cups, fill 2/3 of the cups
5. Bake for 18-20 minutes at 375 F
6. When ready remove from the oven and serve

CRANBERRIES MUFFINS

Serves: **8-12**
Prep Time: **10**   Minutes

Cook Time: **20**   Minutes

Total Time: **30**   Minutes

INGREDIENTS

- 2 eggs
- 1 tablespoon olive oil
- 1 cup milk
- 2 cups whole wheat flour
- 1 tsp baking soda
- ¼ tsp baking soda
- 1 tsp cinnamon
- 1 cup cranberries

DIRECTIONS

1. In a bowl combine all wet ingredients
2. In another bowl combine all dry ingredients
3. Combine wet and dry ingredients together
4. Pour mixture into 8-12 prepared muffin cups, fill 2/3 of the cups
5. Bake for 18-20 minutes at 375 F
6. When ready remove from the oven and serve

COCONUT MUFFINS

Serves: *8-12*
Prep Time: *10*   Minutes

Cook Time: *20*   Minutes

Total Time: *30*   Minutes

INGREDIENTS

- 2 eggs
- 1 tablespoon olive oil
- 1 cup milk
- 2 cups whole wheat flour
- 1 tsp baking soda
- ¼ tsp baking soda
- 1 tsp cinnamon
- 1 cup coconut flakes

DIRECTIONS

1. In a bowl combine all wet ingredients
2. In another bowl combine all dry ingredients
3. Combine wet and dry ingredients together
4. Pour mixture into 8-12 prepared muffin cups, fill 2/3 of the cups
5. Bake for 18-20 minutes at 375 F
6. When ready remove from the oven and serve

OMELETTE

Serves: *1*
Prep Time: 5   Minutes

Cook Time: *10*   Minutes

Total Time: *15*   Minutes

INGREDIENTS

- 2 eggs
- ¼ tsp salt
- ¼ tsp black pepper
- 1 tablespoon olive oil
- ¼ cup cheese
- ¼ tsp basil
- 1 cup cooked chicken breast

DIRECTIONS

1. In a bowl combine all ingredients together and mix well
2. In a skillet heat olive oil and pour the egg mixture
3. Cook for 1-2 minutes per side
4. When ready remove omelette from the skillet and serve

PUMPKIN OMELETTE

Serves: **1**

Prep Time: **5**   Minutes

Cook Time: **10**   Minutes

Total Time: **15**   Minutes

INGREDIENTS

- 2 eggs
- ¼ tsp salt
- ¼ tsp black pepper
- 1 tablespoon olive oil
- ¼ cup cheese
- ¼ tsp basil
- 1 cup pumpkin puree
- 1 cup cooked chicken breast

DIRECTIONS

1. In a bowl combine all ingredients together and mix well
2. In a skillet heat olive oil and pour the egg mixture
3. Cook for 1-2 minutes per side
4. When ready remove omelette from the skillet and serve

SNOW PEAS OMELETTE

Serves: *1*

Prep Time: *5*   Minutes

Cook Time: *10*   Minutes

Total Time: *15*   Minutes

INGREDIENTS

- 2 eggs
- ¼ tsp salt
- ¼ tsp black pepper
- 1 tablespoon olive oil
- ¼ cup cheese
- ¼ tsp basil
- 1 cup chicken breast
- ½ cup snow peas

DIRECTIONS

1. In a bowl combine all ingredients together and mix well
2. In a skillet heat olive oil and pour the egg mixture
3. Cook for 1-2 minutes per side
4. When ready remove omelette from the skillet and serve

Serves: **1**

Prep Time: **5** Minutes

Cook Time: **10** Minutes

Total Time: **15** Minutes

INGREDIENTS

- 2 eggs
- ¼ tsp salt
- ¼ tsp black pepper
- 1 tablespoon olive oil
- ¼ cup cheese
- 1 cup turkey breast
- ¼ tsp basil
- 1 cup mushrooms

DIRECTIONS

1. In a bowl combine all ingredients together and mix well
2. In a skillet heat olive oil and pour the egg mixture
3. Cook for 1-2 minutes per side
4. When ready remove omelette from the skillet and serve

RADISHES OMELETTE

Serves: **1**

Prep Time: **5**   Minutes

Cook Time: **10**   Minutes

Total Time: **15**   Minutes

INGREDIENTS

- 2 eggs
- ¼ tsp salt
- ¼ tsp black pepper
- 1 tablespoon olive oil
- ¼ cup cheese
- 1 cup turkey breast
- ¼ tsp basil
- ½ cup radishes

DIRECTIONS

1. In a bowl combine all ingredients together and mix well
2. In a skillet heat olive oil and pour the egg mixture
3. Cook for 1-2 minutes per side
4. When ready remove omelette from the skillet and serve

BEANS OMELETTE

Serves: **1**

Prep Time: **5**   Minutes

Cook Time: **10**   Minutes

Total Time: **15**   Minutes

INGREDIENTS

- 2 eggs
- ¼ tsp salt
- ¼ tsp black pepper
- 1 tablespoon olive oil
- ¼ cup cheese
- ¼ tsp basil
- 1 cup beans

DIRECTIONS

1. In a bowl combine all ingredients together and mix well
2. In a skillet heat olive oil and pour the egg mixture
3. Cook for 1-2 minutes per side
4. When ready remove omelette from the skillet and serve

BREAKFAST GRANOLA

Serves: 2

Prep Time: 5   Minutes

Cook Time: *30*   Minutes

Total Time: *35*   Minutes

INGREDIENTS

- 1 tsp vanilla extract
- 1 tablespoon honey
- 1 lb. rolled oats
- 2 tablespoons sesame seeds
- ¼ lb. almonds
- ¼ lb. berries

DIRECTIONS

1. Preheat the oven to 325 F
2. Spread the granola onto a baking sheet
3. Bake for 12-15 minutes, remove and mix everything
4. Bake for another 12-15 minutes or until slightly brown
5. When ready remove from the oven and serve

Serves: **1**

Prep Time: **5**   Minutes

Cook Time: **5**   Minutes

Total Time: **10**   Minutes

INGREDIENTS

- ½ cup dried raisins
- ½ cup dried pecans
- ¼ cup almonds
- 1 cup coconut milk
- 1 tsp cinnamon

DIRECTIONS

1. In a bowl combine all ingredients together
2. Serve with milk

SAUSAGE BREAKFAST SANDWICH

Serves: 2

Prep Time: 5   Minutes

Cook Time: 15   Minutes

Total Time: 20   Minutes

INGREDIENTS

- ¼ cup egg substitute
- 1 muffin
- 1 turkey sausage patty
- 1 tablespoon cheddar cheese

DIRECTIONS

1. In a skillet pour egg and cook on low heat
2. Place turkey sausage patty in a pan and cook for 4-5 minutes per side
3. On a toasted muffin place the cooked egg, top with a sausage patty and cheddar cheese
4. Serve when ready

Serves: *8-12*

Prep Time: *10*   Minutes

Cook Time: *20*   Minutes

Total Time: *30*   Minutes

INGREDIENTS

- 2 eggs
- 1 tablespoon olive oil
- 1 cup milk
- 2 cups whole wheat flour
- 1 tsp baking soda
- ¼ tsp baking soda
- 1 tsp cinnamon
- 1 cup strawberries

DIRECTIONS

1. In a bowl combine all wet ingredients
2. In another bowl combine all dry ingredients
3. Combine wet and dry ingredients together
4. Pour mixture into 8-12 prepared muffin cups, fill 2/3 of the cups
5. Bake for 18-20 minutes at 375 F
6. When ready remove from the oven and serve

BUTTERNUT FRITATTA

Serves: 2

Prep Time: *10*   Minutes

Cook Time: *20*   Minutes

Total Time: *30*   Minutes

INGREDIENTS

- ½ lb. butternut
- 1 tablespoon olive oil
- ½ red onion
- 2 eggs
- ¼ tsp salt
- 2 oz. cheddar cheese
- 1 garlic clove
- ¼ tsp dill

DIRECTIONS

1. In a bowl whisk eggs with salt and cheese
2. In a frying pan heat olive oil and pour egg mixture
3. Add remaining ingredients and mix well
4. Serve when ready

Serves: **2**

Prep Time: **10** Minutes

Cook Time: **20** Minutes

Total Time: **30** Minutes

INGREDIENTS

- ½ lb. spinach
- 1 tablespoon olive oil
- ½ red onion
- 2 eggs
- ¼ tsp salt
- 2 oz. cheddar cheese
- 1 garlic clove
- ¼ tsp dill
- 1 tablespoon coriander

DIRECTIONS

1. In a bowl whisk eggs with salt and cheese
2. In a frying pan heat olive oil and pour egg mixture
3. Add remaining ingredients and mix well
4. Serve when ready

DILL FRITATTA

Serves: **2**

Prep Time: **10** Minutes

Cook Time: **20** Minutes

Total Time: **30** Minutes

INGREDIENTS

- 1 tablespoon olive oil
- ½ red onion
- ¼ tsp salt
- 2 eggs
- 2 oz. cheddar cheese
- 1 garlic clove
- 1 tsp dill

DIRECTIONS

1. In a bowl whisk eggs with salt and cheese
2. In a frying pan heat olive oil and pour egg mixture
3. Add remaining ingredients and mix well
4. Serve when ready

PROSCIUTTO FRITATTA

Serves: **2**

Prep Time: **10** Minutes

Cook Time: **20** Minutes

Total Time: **30** Minutes

INGREDIENTS

- 8-10 slices prosciutto
- 1 tablespoon olive oil
- ½ red onion
- ¼ tsp salt
- 2 eggs
- 2 oz. parmesan cheese
- 1 garlic clove
- ¼ tsp dill

DIRECTIONS

1. In a bowl whisk eggs with salt and parmesan cheese
2. In a frying pan heat olive oil and pour egg mixture
3. Add remaining ingredients and mix well
4. When prosciutto and eggs are cooked remove from heat and serve

PEA FRITATTA

Serves: *2*

Prep Time: *10* Minutes

Cook Time: *20* Minutes

Total Time: *30* Minutes

INGREDIENTS

- ½ lb. pea
- 1 tablespoon olive oil
- ½ red onion
- ¼ tsp salt
- 2 oz. cheddar cheese
- 1 garlic clove
- 2 eggs
- ¼ tsp dill

DIRECTIONS

1. In a bowl whisk eggs with salt and cheese
2. In a frying pan heat olive oil and pour egg mixture
3. Add remaining ingredients and mix well
4. Serve when ready

DESSERTS

BREAKFAST COOKIES

Serves: **8-12**

Prep Time: **5** Minutes

Cook Time: **15** Minutes

Total Time: **20** Minutes

INGREDIENTS

- 1 cup rolled oats
- ¼ cup applesauce
- ½ tsp vanilla extract
- 3 tablespoons chocolate chips
- 2 tablespoons dried fruits
- 1 tsp cinnamon

DIRECTIONS

1. Preheat the oven to 325 F
2. In a bowl combine all ingredients together and mix well
3. Scoop cookies using an ice cream scoop
4. Place cookies onto a prepared baking sheet
5. Place in the oven for 12-15 minutes or until the cookies are done
6. When ready remove from the oven and serve

PISTACHIOS ICE-CREAM

Serves: **6-8**

Prep Time: **15** Minutes

Cook Time: **15** Minutes

Total Time: **30** Minutes

INGREDIENTS

- 4 egg yolks
- 1 cup heavy cream
- 1 cup milk
- 1 cup sugar
- 1 vanilla bean
- 1 tsp almond extract
- 1 cup cherries
- ½ cup pistachios

DIRECTIONS

1. In a saucepan whisk together all ingredients
2. Mix until bubbly
3. Strain into a bowl and cool
4. Whisk in favorite fruits and mix well
5. Cover and refrigerate for 2-3 hours
6. Pour mixture in the ice-cream maker and follow manufacturer instructions

VANILLA ICE-CREAM

Serves: *6-8*

Prep Time: *15*   Minutes
Cook Time: *15*   Minutes
Total Time: *30*   Minutes

INGREDIENTS

- 1 cup milk
- 1 tablespoon cornstarch
- 1 oz. cream cheese
- 1 cup heavy cream
- 1 cup brown sugar
- 1 tablespoon corn syrup
- 1 vanilla bean

DIRECTIONS

1. In a saucepan whisk together all ingredients
2. Mix until bubbly
3. Strain into a bowl and cool
4. Whisk in favorite fruits and mix well
5. Cover and refrigerate for 2-3 hours
6. Pour mixture in the ice-cream maker and follow manufacturer instructions
7. Serve when ready

COFFE ICE-CREAM

Serves: **6-8**

Prep Time: **15**   Minutes

Cook Time: **15**   Minutes

Total Time: **30**   Minutes

INGREDIENTS

- 4 egg yolks
- 1 cup black coffee
- 2 cups heavy cream
- 1 cup half-and-half
- 1 cup brown sugar
- 1 tsp vanilla extract

DIRECTIONS

1. In a saucepan whisk together all ingredients
2. Mix until bubbly
3. Strain into a bowl and cool
4. Whisk in favorite fruits and mix well
5. Cover and refrigerate for 2-3 hours
6. Pour mixture in the ice-cream maker and follow manufacturer instructions
7. Serve when ready

STRAWBERRY ICE-CREAM

Serves: **6-8**

Prep Time: **15**   Minutes
Cook Time: **15**   Minutes
Total Time: **30**   Minutes

INGREDIENTS

- 1 lb. strawberries
- ½ cup sugar
- 1 tablespoon vanilla extract
- 1 cup heavy cram
- 1-pint vanilla

DIRECTIONS

1. In a saucepan whisk together all ingredients
2. Mix until bubbly
3. Strain into a bowl and cool
4. Whisk in favorite fruits and mix well
5. Cover and refrigerate for 2-3 hours
6. Pour mixture in the ice-cream maker and follow manufacturer instructions
7. Serve when ready

WATERMELON SMOOTHIE

Serves: **1**

Prep Time: 5   Minutes

Cook Time: 5   Minutes

Total Time: **10**   Minutes

INGREDIENTS

- 2 cups watermelon
- 1 cup almond milk
- 1 cup vanilla yogurt
- 2 tablespoons maple syrup
- 1 cup ice

DIRECTIONS

1. In a blender place all ingredients and blend until smooth
2. Pour smoothie in a glass and serve

COCONUT SMOOTHIE

Serves: *1*

Prep Time: *5*   Minutes

Cook Time: *5*   Minutes

Total Time: *10*   Minutes

INGREDIENTS

- 2 cup pineapple
- ¼ cup coconut milk
- 1 cup pineapple juice
- 2 tablespoons coconut flakes
- ½ cup yogurt
- 1 tablespoon honey

DIRECTIONS

1. In a blender place all ingredients and blend until smooth
2. Pour smoothie in a glass and serve

STRAWBERRY BANANA SMOOTHIE

Serves: *1*

Prep Time: *5*   Minutes

Cook Time: *5*   Minutes

Total Time: *10* Minutes

INGREDIENTS

- 1 cup raspberries
- 1 cup strawberries
- 1 banana
- 1 cup almond milk
- 1 tablespoon honey
- 1 cup ice

DIRECTIONS

1. In a blender place all ingredients and blend until smooth
2. Pour smoothie in a glass and serve

BASIC SMOOTHIE

Serves: **1**
Prep Time: **5** Minutes

Cook Time: **5** Minutes

Total Time: **10** Minutes

INGREDIENTS

- 1 apple
- 1 pear
- 1 cup coconut water
- 1 tablespoon honey

DIRECTIONS

1. In a blender place all ingredients and blend until smooth
2. Pour smoothie in a glass and serve

Serves: *1*

Prep Time: 5   Minutes

Cook Time: 5   Minutes

Total Time: *10* Minutes

INGREDIENTS

- 1 avocado
- 1 cup spinach
- 1 banana
- ½ cup cauliflower
- 2 dates
- 1 cup almond milk

DIRECTIONS

1. In a blender place all ingredients and blend until smooth
2. Pour smoothie in a glass and serve

Serves: **1**

Prep Time: **5** Minutes

Cook Time: **5** Minutes

Total Time: **10** Minutes

INGREDIENTS

- 1 cup strawberries
- 1 banana
- 1 cup Greek Yogurt
- 1 cup orange juice

DIRECTIONS

1. In a blender place all ingredients and blend until smooth
2. Pour smoothie in a glass and serve

PEANUT BUTTER SMOOTHIE

Serves: **1**

Prep Time: 5   Minutes

Cook Time: 5   Minutes

Total Time: **10**   Minutes

INGREDIENTS

- 2 cups banana
- 1 tablespoon flax seeds
- 1 cup almond milk
- 1 tsp vanilla extract
- 2 tablespoon peanut butter

DIRECTIONS

1. In a blender place all ingredients and blend until smooth
2. Pour smoothie in a glass and serve

SPINACH SMOOTHIE

Serves: *1*
Prep Time: *5*   Minutes

Cook Time: *5*   Minutes

Total Time: *10*   Minutes

INGREDIENTS

- 2 cups banana
- 2 cups strawberries
- 2 cups spinach
- 2 chia seeds

DIRECTIONS

1. In a blender place all ingredients and blend until smooth
2. Pour smoothie in a glass and serve

PROTEIN SMOOTHIE

Serves: *1*

Prep Time: 5   Minutes

Cook Time: 5   Minutes

Total Time: *10*   Minutes

INGREDIENTS

- 1 cup berries
- 1 tablespoon chia seeds
- ½ cup protein powder
- 1 cup almond milk

DIRECTIONS

1. In a blender place all ingredients and blend until smooth
2. Pour smoothie in a glass and serve

BREAKFAST SMOOTHIE

Serves: **1**

Prep Time: **5**   Minutes

Cook Time: **5**   Minutes

Total Time: **10** Minutes

INGREDIENTS

- ½ cup oatmeal
- ½ cup protein powder
- 1 tablespoon peanut butter
- 1 cup coconut milk
- 1 banana

DIRECTIONS

1. In a blender place all ingredients and blend until smooth
2. Pour smoothie in a glass and serve

SIXTH COOKBOOK

SOUP RECIPES

MUSHROOM SOUP

Serves: **4**

Prep Time: **10**   Minutes

Cook Time: **20**   Minutes

Total Time: **30**   Minutes

INGREDIENTS

- 1 tablespoon olive oil
- 1 lb. mushrooms
- ¼ red onion
- ½ cup all-purpose flour
- ¼ tsp salt
- ¼ tsp pepper
- 1 can vegetable broth
- 1 cup heavy cream

DIRECTIONS

1. In a saucepan heat olive oil and sauté mushrooms until tender
2. Add remaining ingredients to the saucepan and bring to a boil
3. When all the vegetables are tender transfer to a blender and blend until smooth
4. Pour soup into bowls, garnish with parsley and serve

ZUCCHINI SOUP

Serves: **4**

Prep Time: **10** Minutes

Cook Time: **20** Minutes

Total Time: **30** Minutes

INGREDIENTS

- 1 tablespoon olive oil
- 1 lb. zucchini
- ¼ red onion
- ½ cup all-purpose flour
- ¼ tsp salt
- ¼ tsp pepper
- 1 can vegetable broth
- 1 cup heavy cream

DIRECTIONS

1. In a saucepan heat olive oil and sauté zucchini until tender
2. Add remaining ingredients to the saucepan and bring to a boil
3. When all the vegetables are tender transfer to a blender and blend until smooth
4. Pour soup into bowls, garnish with parsley and serve

SPINACH SOUP

Serves: **4**

Prep Time: **10** Minutes

Cook Time: **20** Minutes

Total Time: **30** Minutes

INGREDIENTS

- 1 tablespoon olive oil
- 1 lb. spinach
- ¼ red onion
- ½ cup all-purpose flour
- ¼ tsp salt
- ¼ tsp pepper
- 1 can vegetable broth
- 1 cup heavy cream

DIRECTIONS

1. In a saucepan heat olive oil and sauté spinach until tender
2. Add remaining ingredients to the saucepan and bring to a boil
3. When all the vegetables are tender transfer to a blender and blend until smooth
4. Pour soup into bowls, garnish with parsley and serve

CARROT SOUP

Serves: **4**

Prep Time: **10** Minutes

Cook Time: **20** Minutes

Total Time: **30** Minutes

INGREDIENTS

- 1 tablespoon olive oil
- 1 lb. carrots
- ¼ red onion
- ½ cup all-purpose flour
- ¼ tsp salt
- ¼ tsp pepper
- 1 can vegetable broth
- 1 cup heavy cream

DIRECTIONS

1. In a saucepan heat olive oil and sauté carrots until tender
2. Add remaining ingredients to the saucepan and bring to a boil
3. When all the vegetables are tender transfer to a blender and blend until smooth
4. Pour soup into bowls, garnish with parsley and serve

Serves: **4**

Prep Time: **10** Minutes

Cook Time: **20** Minutes

Total Time: **30** Minutes

INGREDIENTS

- 1 tablespoon olive oil
- 1 lb. mushrooms
- ¼ red onion
- ½ cup all-purpose flour
- ¼ tsp salt
- ¼ tsp pepper
- 1 can vegetable broth
- 1 cup heavy cream

DIRECTIONS

1. In a saucepan heat olive oil and sauté potatoes until tender
2. Add remaining ingredients to the saucepan and bring to a boil
3. When all the vegetables are tender transfer to a blender and blend until smooth
4. Pour soup into bowls, garnish with parsley and serve

ZUCCHINI SOUP

Serves: *4*

Prep Time: *10* Minutes

Cook Time: *20* Minutes

Total Time: *30* Minutes

INGREDIENTS

- 1 tablespoon olive oil
- 1 lb. zucchini
- ¼ red onion
- ½ cup all-purpose flour
- ¼ tsp salt
- ¼ tsp pepper
- 1 can vegetable broth
- 1 cup heavy cream

DIRECTIONS

1. In a saucepan heat olive oil and sauté zucchini until tender
2. Add remaining ingredients to the saucepan and bring to a boil
3. When all the vegetables are tender transfer to a blender and blend until smooth
4. Pour soup into bowls, garnish with parsley and serve

SIDE DISHES

GREEN PESTO PASTA

Serves: **2**
Prep Time: **5** Minutes

Cook Time: **15** Minutes

Total Time: **20** Minutes

INGREDIENTS

- 4 oz. spaghetti
- 2 cups basil leaves
- 2 garlic cloves
- ¼ cup olive oil
- 2 tablespoons parmesan cheese
- ½ tsp black pepper

DIRECTIONS

1. Bring water to a boil and add pasta
2. In a blend add parmesan cheese, basil leaves, garlic and blend
3. Add olive oil, pepper and blend again
4. Pour pesto onto pasta and serve when ready

BUTTERMILK FRIED CHICKEN

Serves: **4**

Prep Time: **10**   Minutes

Cook Time: **20**   Minutes

Total Time: **30**   Minutes

INGREDIENTS

- 2 chicken breasts
- ½ cup low fat buttermilk
- salt free seasoning
- ¼ cup bread crumbs
- salt

DIRECTIONS

1. Preheat the oven to 400 F
2. Cut chicken breast in half and marinate in buttermilk and seasoning for 45-60 minutes
3. Dredge each piece of chicken in crumbs and coat well
4. Place chicken on a sheet pan and bake for 12-15 minutes or until golden
5. When ready, remove and serve

Serves: **1**

Prep Time: **10** Minutes

Cook Time: **20** Minutes

Total Time: **30** Minutes

INGREDIENTS

- 2 tsp soy sauce
- 2 tsp rice wine vinegar
- 1 tablespoon ginger root
- 5 oz. fillet white fish
- 2 green onions

DIRECTIONS

1. Preheat the oven to 400 F
2. In a bowl mix ginger, rice wine vinegar and soy sauce
3. Place the fish fillet on the parchment paper and top with green onion and drizzle with soy mixture
4. Top with mushrooms, jasmine rice and bake for 10-15 minutes, when ready, remove and serve

Serves: *6*

Prep Time: *10*   Minutes

Cook Time: *1*   Hour 30 Minutes

Total Time: *1*   Hour 40 Minutes

INGREDIENTS

- 5 lbs. turkey breast
- 1 recipe wild mushrooms
- 1 tablespoon maple syrup

DIRECTIONS

1. Preheat the oven to 375 F
2. Place the turkey breast on a butting board and season with salt and pepper
3. Place stuffing in the center of the pan
4. Roast for 1 hour and 30 minutes
5. Remove, brush with maple syrup and allow to rest before serving

GARLIC MASHED POTATOES

Serves: **4**

Prep Time: **10**   Minutes

Cook Time: **30**   Minutes

Total Time: **40**   Minutes

INGREDIENTS

- 6 potatoes
- ½ cup milk
- ½ cup butter
- 1 clove garlic
- 1 pinch of salt
- 1 pinch ground black pepper
- 1 tablespoon sesame seeds

DIRECTIONS

1. In a pot bring water to boil, add potatoes and boil for 25 minutes
2. In a bowl mix pepper, garlic, milk, butter and salt with a hand mixer
3. Sprinkle with sesame seeds and serve with mashed potatoes

STUFFING STOCK

Serves: **6**

Prep Time: **10**   Minutes

Cook Time: **2**   Hours

Total Time: **2**   Hours 10 Minutes

INGREDIENTS

- 6 cups chicken stock
- 2 onions
- 2 stalks celery
- spring parsley
- 1 bay leaf
- 4 peppercorns
- mushroom steams

DIRECTIONS

1. In a pot add all ingredients and cover with a lid
2. Bring mixture to a boil and simmer for 2 hours
3. When ready remove from heat
4. Refrigerate and serve

MOIST ROAST CHICKEN

Serves: **4**

Prep Time: **10**   Minutes

Cook Time: **30**   Minutes

Total Time: **40**   Minutes

INGREDIENTS

- 2 chicken breasts
- salt
- pepper

DIRECTIONS

1. Preheat the oven to 400 F
2. Place chicken breast on a cutting board and season with salt and pepper
3. Roast for 30 minutes
4. Remove and serve when ready

SPINACH FISH ROLLS

Serves: **4**

Prep Time: **10**   Minutes

Cook Time: **20**   Minutes

Total Time: **30**   Minutes

INGREDIENTS

- 1 lb. fillets
- seasoning
- 1 cup spinach
- 1 cup mayonnaise
- plain bread crumbs
- 1 tablespoon white vermouth

DIRECTIONS

1. Preheat the oven to 375 F
2. Season fish fillets with seasoning and chopped spinach
3. Roll fillets and top each roll with mayonnaise and a sprinkle of bread crumbs
4. Add vermouth to the baking dish and bake for 18-20 minutes, remove and serve with lemon wedges

GAU'S CHICKEN

Serves: **4**

Prep Time: **10** Minutes

Cook Time: **20** Minutes

Total Time: **30** Minutes

INGREDIENTS

- 1 tablespoon cornstarch
- ¼ cup water
- 2 garlic cloves
- 2 tsp ginger root
- 2 tablespoons brown sugar
- 2 tablespoons soy sauce
- 1 tablespoon orange juice
- 1 lb. chicken breast

DIRECTIONS

1. In a bowl mix all ingredients except chicken breast
2. Season chicken breast with salt and pepper
3. Sauté chicken in large wok for 2-3 minutes
4. Add cornstarch mixture and cook for another 5-6 minutes
5. When ready, remove from heat and serve

Serves: **4**

Prep Time: **10** Minutes

Cook Time: **30** Minutes

Total Time: **40** Minutes

INGREDIENTS

- 4 eggs

DIRECTIONS

1. Preheat the oven to 300 F
2. In a muffin pan place 4 eggs and cook for 25-30 minutes
3. When eggs are done, transfer to a bowl of cold water, allow to cool, peel and store

WHIPPED SWEET POTATOES

Serves: **6**
Prep Time: **10** Minutes

Cook Time: **60** Minutes

Total Time: **70** Minutes

INGREDIENTS

- 2 lbs. sweet potatoes
- ½ cup orange juice
- ¼ cup water
- 1 tablespoon coconut oil
- 1 tsp cinnamon
- 1 tsp salt

DIRECTIONS

1. Preheat the oven to 350 F
2. Place sweet potatoes on a baking sheet
3. Bake for 50-60 minutes, remove and slice each potato in half
4. Add all ingredients in a blender, blend until smooth and serve

BUTTERNUT SQUASH RISSOTTO

Serves: **4**

Prep Time: **10** Minutes

Cook Time: **20** Minutes

Total Time: **30** Minutes

INGREDIENTS

- 1 cup uncooked rice
- 1 tsp olive oil
- 2 cups chicken broth
- 1 cup butternut squash
- 1 pinch of salt
- 1 pinch of black pepper
- 5 tablespoons Parmesan cheese

DIRECTIONS

1. In a bowl mix rice, oil and microwave for 3-4 minutes
2. Add broth, water and microwave for 8-10 minutes
3. Add salt, pepper, squash, cheese risotto and stir well
4. Serve when ready

BUTTERNUT SQUASH STEW

Serves: **4**

Prep Time: **10**   Minutes

Cook Time: **30**   Minutes

Total Time: **40**   Minutes

INGREDIENTS

- 2 tsp olive oil
- 1 clove garlic
- 2 cups butternut squash
- 1 cup carrots
- 2 cups chicken broth
- ¼ tsp thyme
- 1 bay leaf
- ½ tsp salt
- 8 oz. chicken breast
- ¼ tsp onion powder
- 1 pinch nutmeg
- 1 tablespoon orange juice concentrate

DIRECTIONS

1. In a Dutch oven add garlic, olive oil, carrots, squash cubes and cook for 4-5 minutes
2. Stir in thyme, salt, bay leaf, broth and bring to a boil

3. Simmer for 15-20 minutes, until vegetables are tender

4. Remove 1 cup and puree, return to the pan and bring to a boil

5. Add chicken cubes, orange juice, nutmeg and simmer for another 5-6 minutes

6. When ready, remove from heat and serve

Serves: **2**

Prep Time: 5   Minutes

Cook Time: 5   Minutes

Total Time: **10**   Minutes

INGREDIENTS

- 1 cup broccoli
- 1 cup quinoa
- 2 radishes
- 2 tablespoons pumpkin seeds
- 1 cup salad dressing

DIRECTIONS

1. In a bowl mix all ingredients and mix well
2. Serve with dressing

Serves: *2*

Prep Time: 5   Minutes

Cook Time: 5   Minutes

Total Time: *10*   Minutes

INGREDIENTS

- 2 carrots
- 2 purple carrots
- 1 cabbage
- ¼ red onion
- 1 bunch leaves
- 2 kale leaves
- 1 cup salad dressing

DIRECTIONS

1. In a bowl mix all ingredients and mix well

2. Serve with dressing

MINT SALAD

Serves: 2
Prep Time: 5   Minutes

Cook Time: 5   Minutes

Total Time: 10   Minutes

INGREDIENTS

- 1 lb. broad beans
- ½ lb. peas
- 2 chives
- Mint leaves
- 2 spring onions
- 2 tablespoons olive oil
- 2 tablespoons lemon juice

DIRECTIONS

1. In a bowl mix all ingredients and mix well
2. Serve with dressing

Serves: 2

Prep Time: 5   Minutes

Cook Time: 5   Minutes

Total Time: **10**   Minutes

INGREDIENTS

- 1 bunch coriander leaves
- 1 bunch mint leaves
- ¼ red onion
- 1 bunch parsley
- 1 cup lentils
- 1 tablespoon pumpkin seeds
- 1 tablespoon pine nuts

DIRECTIONS

1. In a bowl mix all ingredients and mix well
2. Serve with dressing

CAULIFLOWER SALAD

Serves: **2**

Prep Time: **5** Minutes

Cook Time: **5** Minutes

Total Time: **10** Minutes

INGREDIENTS

- 1 cauliflower
- 4 slices bacon
- ¼ cup sour cream
- ¼ cup mayonnaise
- 1 tablespoon lemon juice
- ¼ tsp garlic powder
- 1 cup cheddar cheese
- ¼ cup chives

DIRECTIONS

1. In a bowl mix all ingredients and mix well
2. Serve with dressing

Serves: 2

Prep Time: 5   Minutes

Cook Time: 5   Minutes

Total Time: **10** Minutes

INGREDIENTS

- 1 cup buffalo sauce
- 1 tablespoon lime juice
- 1 tsp garlic powder
- ¼ tsp onion powder
- 1 lb. cooked chicken breast
- 1 tablespoon olive oil

DIRECTIONS

1. In a bowl mix all ingredients and mix well
2. Serve with dressing

Serves: **2**

Prep Time: **10** Minutes

Cook Time: **20** Minutes

Total Time: **30** Minutes

INGREDIENTS

- ½ lb. watercress
- 1 tablespoon olive oil
- ½ red onion
- 2 eggs
- ½ cup salami
- ¼ tsp salt
- 2 oz. cheddar cheese
- 1 garlic clove
- ¼ tsp dill

DIRECTIONS

1. In a skillet sauté onion until tender
2. In a bowl whisk eggs with salt and cheese
3. In a frying pan heat olive oil and pour egg mixture
4. Add remaining ingredients and mix well
5. Serve when ready

SQUASH FRITATTA

Serves: 2

Prep Time: **10** Minutes

Cook Time: **20** Minutes

Total Time: **30** Minutes

INGREDIENTS

- ½ cup spaghetti squash
- 1 tablespoon olive oil
- ½ red onion
- ¼ tsp salt
- 2 eggs
- 2 oz. parmesan cheese
- 1 garlic clove
- ½ cup salami
- ¼ tsp dill

DIRECTIONS

1. In a bowl whisk eggs with salt and parmesan cheese
2. In a frying pan heat olive oil and pour egg mixture
3. Add remaining ingredients and mix well
4. Serve when ready

BROCCOLI FRITATTA

Serves: 2

Prep Time: **10**   Minutes

Cook Time: **20**   Minutes

Total Time: **30**   Minutes

INGREDIENTS

- 1 cup broccoli
- 1 tablespoon olive oil
- 2 eggs
- ½ red onion
- ¼ tsp salt
- ½ cup salami
- 2 oz. cheddar cheese
- 1 garlic clove
- ¼ tsp dill

DIRECTIONS

1. In a skillet sauté broccoli until tender
2. In a bowl whisk eggs with salt and cheese
3. In a frying pan heat olive oil and pour egg mixture
4. Add remaining ingredients and mix well
5. When ready serve with sautéed broccoli

Serves: *2*

Prep Time: *10* Minutes

Cook Time: *30* Minutes

Total Time: *40* Minutes

INGREDIENTS

- 2 chicken breasts
- 1 tsp garlic powder
- 1 tablespoon butter
- 2 tablespoons olive oil
- 1 tsp salt

DIRECTIONS

1. Place the chicken breast in a baking dish
2. Rub with garlic powder, garlic, salt and olive oil
3. Bake at 350 F for 28-30 minutes
4. When ready remove from the oven and serve

Serves: 2

Prep Time: *10*   Minutes

Cook Time: *8*   Hours

Total Time: *8*   Hours 10 Minutes

INGREDIENTS

- 2 lb. pork shoulder
- 1 tablespoon salt
- 1 tablespoon ginger powder
- 1 tablespoon peppercorns

DIRECTIONS

1. Place the pork in a slow cooker
2. Sprinkle with ginger powder, salt and peppercorns
3. Cook on low heat for 7-8 hours
4. When ready remove from the slow cooker and serve

Serves: **4**

Prep Time: **10**   Minutes

Cook Time: **20**   Minutes

Total Time: **30**   Minutes

INGREDIENTS

- 2 lb. pork tenderloin
- 1 tsp salt
- 1 tsp pepper
- 1 tsp coriander
- 1 tsp oregano
- 2 tablespoons olive oil

DIRECTIONS

1. Cut the pork tenderloin in half
2. Sprinkle with spices and rub the pork the pork
3. In a frying pan heat olive oil and place the pork tenderloin
4. Cook the pork on both sides
5. When ready remove from heat and serve

DOVER SOLE FILLETS

Serves: **2**

Prep Time: **10**   Minutes

Cook Time: **10**   Minutes

Total Time: **20**   Minutes

INGREDIENTS

- 4 dover sole fillets
- ½ cup olive oil
- 2 cardamom pods
- 1 cup cilantro leaves
- 1 tsp salt

DIRECTIONS

1. Place the cilantro, lemon zest, cardamom pods and olive oil in a proof dish
2. Lay the filets in the dish and sprinkle with salt
3. Broil on high for 8-10 minutes
4. When ready remove and serve

ROASTED SALMON

Serves: **4**

Prep Time: **10**   Minutes

Cook Time: **25**   Minutes

Total Time: **35**   Minutes

INGREDIENTS

- 2 lb. salmon fillets
- 2 tablespoons olive oil
- ½ tsp salt
- ¼ tsp oregano
- ¼ tsp thyme
- ½ tsp cumin

DIRECTIONS

1. Place the salmon fillet on a baking sheet
2. Season with salt, herbs and spices
3. Bake at 400 F for 22-25 minutes
4. When ready remove from the oven and serve

LIME STEAK

Serves: **2**

Prep Time: **10** Minutes

Cook Time: **20** Minutes

Total Time: **30** Minutes

INGREDIENTS

- ½ cup olive oil
- 2-3 tablespoons lime juice
- Zest of ½ lime
- 1 tablespoon garlic
- 1 tsp ginger
- 2 lb. grass-fed steak

DIRECTIONS

1. In a bowl combine lime juice, olive oil, garlic, ginger and mix well
2. Rub the steak with the marinade and let it marinade for 20-30 minutes
3. Transfer skillet to a skillet
4. Cook for 3-4 minutes per side
5. When ready remove from the skillet and serve

GARLIC BISON ROAST

Serves: 2

Prep Time: **10** Minutes

Cook Time: **60** Minutes

Total Time: **70** Minutes

INGREDIENTS

- 2 lb. grass fed bison roast
- 2 cloves garlic
- ¼ tsp oregano
- ¼ tsp thyme
- 1 tsp sage
- 2-3 tsp olive oil

DIRECTIONS

1. In a bowl combine garlic, oregano, thyme, sage and olive oil together
2. Place the bison roast in the marinade and let it marinade overnight
3. Roast at 425 F for 18-20 minutes
4. Reduce the heat at 250 F and cook for another 40-45 minutes
5. When ready remove to a cutting board
6. Slice and serve

Serves: 2

Prep Time: **10** Minutes

Cook Time: **30** Minutes

Total Time: **40** Minutes

INGREDIENTS

- 4 bone marrow halves
- 1 tsp salt
- 1 tsp parsley

DIRECTIONS

1. Place the bones on a baking tray
2. Sprinkle salt and parsley
3. Bake at 350 F for 28-30 minutes
4. When marrow is golden brown remove from the oven and serve

ROASTED CHICKEN LIVER

Serves: *1*
Prep Time: *5*   Minutes

Cook Time: *15*   Minutes

Total Time: *20*   Minutes

INGREDIENTS

- 1 lb. chicken liver
- 2 tablespoons olive oil
- 1 lemon
- 2 cloves garlic
- 1 tsp salt
- 1 tsp thyme

DIRECTIONS

1. Heat olive oil in a skillet
2. Add garlic, salt and thyme, cook for 2-3 minutes
3. Place the chicken liver in the skillet
4. Cook for 5-6 minutes
5. When ready remove from the skillet and serve

PIZZA

CHICKEN PIZZA

Serves: *6-8*

Prep Time: *10*   Minutes

Cook Time: *15*   Minutes

Total Time: *25*   Minutes

INGREDIENTS

- 1 cup cooked chicken breast
- ½ cup bbq sauce
- 1 pizza crust
- 1 tablespoon olive oil
- 1 cup cheese
- 1 cup tomatoes

DIRECTIONS

1. Spread tomato sauce on the pizza crust
2. Place all the toppings on the pizza crust
3. Bake the pizza at 425 F for 12-15 minutes
4. When ready remove pizza from the oven and serve

Serves: **6-8**

Prep Time: **10** Minutes

Cook Time: **15** Minutes

Total Time: **25** Minutes

INGREDIENTS

- 1 pizza crust
- 1 tablespoon garlic
- 1 tsp salt
- 2-3 tomatoes
- 1 pizza crust
- 4 oz. mozzarella cheese
- 6-8 basil leaves
- ¼ cup parmesan cheese
- ¼ cup feta cheese

DIRECTIONS

1. Spread tomato sauce on the pizza crust
2. Place all the toppings on the pizza crust
3. Bake the pizza at 425 F for 12-15 minutes
4. When ready remove pizza from the oven and serve

VEGGIE PIZZA

Serves: **6-8**

Prep Time: **10**   Minutes

Cook Time: **15**   Minutes

Total Time: **25**   Minutes

INGREDIENTS

- 1 cup sour cream
- 1 tsp dill
- ¼ tsp salt
- ½ red onion
- 1 red bell pepper
- 1 cup broccoli
- 1 carrot

DIRECTIONS

1. Spread tomato sauce on the pizza crust
2. Place all the toppings on the pizza crust
3. Bake the pizza at 425 F for 12-15 minutes
4. When ready remove pizza from the oven and serve

SPINACH PITA PIZZA

Serves: **4**

Prep Time: **10** Minutes

Cook Time: **20** Minutes

Total Time: **30** Minutes

INGREDIENTS

- 1 white pizza
- strained pizza sauce
- 1 tablespoon Italian seasoning
- 1 tablespoon spinach
- ½ cup cottage cheese
- 1 oz. mozzarella cheese

DIRECTIONS

1. Preheat the oven to 375 F
2. Toast pita and spread tomato space over
3. Sprinkle with seasoning, spinach, mozzarella and cottage cheese
4. Return to oven and bake until cheese is fully melted
5. When ready, remove from oven and serve

SEVENTH COOKBOOK

ROAST RECIPES

ROASTED TOMATO

Serves: **3-4**

Prep Time: **10**   Minutes

Cook Time: **20**   Minutes

Total Time: **30**   Minutes

INGREDIENTS

- 1 lb. tomatoes
- 2 tablespoons olive oil
- 1 tsp curry powder
- 1 tsp salt

DIRECTIONS

1. Preheat the oven to 400 F
2. Cut everything in half lengthwise
3. Toss everything with olive oil and place onto a prepared baking sheet
4. Roast for 18-20 minutes at 400 F or until golden brown
5. When ready remove from the oven and serve

Serves: *3-4*
Prep Time: *10*   Minutes

Cook Time: *20*   Minutes

Total Time: *30*   Minutes

INGREDIENTS

- 2 delicata squashes
- 2 tablespoons olive oil
- 1 tsp curry powder
- 1 tsp salt

DIRECTIONS

1. Preheat the oven to 400 F
2. Cut everything in half lengthwise
3. Toss everything with olive oil and place onto a prepared baking sheet
4. Roast for 18-20 minutes at 400 F or until golden brown
5. When ready remove from the oven and serve

ROASTED EGGPLANT

Serves: **4**

Prep Time: **10** Minutes

Cook Time: **45** Minutes

Total Time: **55** Minutes

INGREDIENTS

- 2 eggplants
- 1 tablespoon olive oil
- 5 olives
- 2 cups canned cannellini
- 1 anchovy fillets
- 1 tablespoon lemon juice
- 1 tsp salt
- 1 cloves garlic
- ¼ chopped fresh parsley
- 2 dried tomatoes

DIRECTIONS

1. Roast the eggplant in oven at 375 F for 40 minutes
2. In a blender add garlic and eggplant and add olive oil, parsley, tomato, beans, olives and lemon juice

Blend mixture until smooth remove and serve

ZUCCHINI SOUP

Serves: **4**

Prep Time: **10**   Minutes

Cook Time: **20**   Minutes

Total Time: **30**   Minutes

INGREDIENTS

- 1 tablespoon olive oil
- 1 lb. zucchini
- ¼ red onion
- ½ cup all-purpose flour
- ¼ tsp salt
- ¼ tsp pepper
- 1 can vegetable broth
- 1 cup heavy cream

DIRECTIONS

1. In a saucepan heat olive oil and sauté zucchini until tender
2. Add remaining ingredients to the saucepan and bring to a boil
3. When all the vegetables are tender transfer to a blender and blend until smooth
4. Pour soup into bowls, garnish with parsley and serve

CHIPOTLE BEAN SOUP

Serves: 2

Prep Time: *10* Minutes

Cook Time: *20* Minutes

Total Time: *30* Minutes

INGREDIENTS

- ½ small onion
- 2 tsp olive oil
- 1 clove garlic
- 2 cups chicken broth
- ¼ chipotle chili powder
- baby carrots

DIRECTIONS

1. In a saucepan sauce onion with olive oil for 2-3 minutes over medium heat
2. Add beans, garlic, chili powder and vegetable broth
3. Add baby carrots and simmer for 12-15 minutes
4. Pure the mixture and season with salt

SIDE DISHES

SPINACH SPREAD

Serves: **4**
Prep Time: **10**   Minutes

Cook Time: **20**   Minutes

Total Time: **30**   Minutes

INGREDIENTS

- 2 tsp canola oil
- ½ tsp lemon zest
- ½ tsp pepper
- ¼ grated nutmeg
- ½ cup water
- 2 10-ounce packages frozen spinach
- 1-ounce parmesan cheese
- 1 cup cottage cheese
- 2 tablespoons lemon juice
- 1 cup onion
- 2 cloves garlic

DIRECTIONS

1. In a skillet heat oil over medium heat and add garlic and onion
2. Cook for 7-8 minutes an add water and spinach

3. Transfer mixture in a blender and add parmesan cheese, lemon juice, cottage cheese, pepper, lemon zest, nutmeg, salt and puree until smooth

4. Refrigerate at least 4h before serving

LENTIL HUMMUS

Serves: *6*
Prep Time: *10* Minutes

Cook Time: *30* Minutes

Total Time: *40* Minutes

INGREDIENTS

- 1 15-ounce can lentils
- ¼ tsp salt
- ¼ ground cumin
- ¼ cup water
- ½ cup sesame tahini
- 1 clove garlic
- ¼ cup olive oil
- 2 tablespoons lemon juice

DIRECTIONS

1. Mix all the ingredients except water in a blender and blend until smooth
2. Remove and serve

CUMIN SCENTED BEAN DIP

Serves: *4*

Prep Time: *10* Minutes

Cook Time: *10* Minutes

Total Time: *20* Minutes

INGREDIENTS

- 2 tablespoons olive oil
- ½ cup plain yogurt
- ½ tsp cumin
- ¼ tsp garlic
- pepper
- salt
- white beans

DIRECTIONS

1. In a blender add olive oil, white beans, cumin, yogurt, garlic and blend until smooth
2. Season with pepper or salt and serve with cucumber slices or pita

BEAN AND CORN TACOS

Serves: **2**

Prep Time: **10**   Minutes

Cook Time: **20**   Minutes

Total Time: **30**   Minutes

INGREDIENTS

- Beans
- ½ cup corn salsa
- baby spinach
- ½ avocado

DIRECTIONS

1. In a saucepan mix beans with salsa
2. Simmer for 12-15 minutes and serve with tortillas and a pinch of cheese

BLACK BEAN SALAD WITH QUINOA

Serves: *2*

Prep Time: *10* Minutes

Cook Time: *20* Minutes

Total Time: *30* Minutes

INGREDIENTS

- ¼ cup dried quino
- 1 cup butternut squash
- 2 tablespoons water
- ¼ crumbled feta cheese
- 2 tablespoons cilantro
- salt

DIRECTIONS

1. In a saucepan add quinoa, squash and water and simmer for 12-15 minutes until squash is cooked
2. Stir in beans and feta cheese and cilantro
3. Remove from heat and season with salt

CREAMY SCRAMBLED EGGS

Serves: **2**

Prep Time: **10** Minutes

Cook Time: **30** Minutes

Total Time: **40** Minutes

INGREDIENTS

- 2 tablespoons milk
- salt
- 3 eggs
- 1/3 cup low fat cheese

DIRECTIONS

1. Beat the eggs with milk and salt
2. Cook in a nonstick pan over medium heat
3. Stir in cottage cheese remove and serve

CHICKEN CURRY WITH BROWN RICE

Serves: *2*

Prep Time: *10* Minutes

Cook Time: *20* Minutes

Total Time: *30* Minutes

INGREDIENTS

- 1 cup brown rice
- coconut milk
- 1 tsp curry paste
- vegetable mix

DIRECTIONS

1. In a saucepan simmer sliced vegetables in coconut milk and chicken and add Thai curry paste
2. Remove and serve over brown rice

Serves: 2

Prep Time: *10*   Minutes

Cook Time: *20*   Minutes

Total Time: *30*   Minutes

INGREDIENTS

- Brown rice
- Black beans
- 1 avocado
- 1 cup lettuce
- 1 cup shredded cheese

DIRECTIONS

1. Top brown rice with avocado, lettuce, beans and shredded cheese and serve

LEMON ROSEMARY CHICKEN

Serves: *4*
Prep Time: *10* Minutes

Cook Time: *30* Minutes

Total Time: *40* Minutes

INGREDIENTS

- 4 6oz. boneless chicken breast
- 2 tsp olive oil
- 1 tsp lemon pepper seasoning
- 1 tsp salt
- 2 lemons
- fresh rosemary
- 1 cup chicken broth
- ½ tsp garlic

DIRECTIONS

1. Preheat oven to 350 F
2. Brush chicken with olive oil and sprinkle with lemon seasoning
3. In a baking dish place chicken with rosemary and top with lemon slices
4. Bake for 20-25 minutes or until golden brown
5. In a saucepan mix rosemary with chicken broth and garlic
6. Serve mixture with chicken and garnish with lemon slice

PAN CON TOMATE

Serves: **4**
Prep Time: **10**   Minutes

Cook Time: **10**   Minutes

Total Time: **20**   Minutes

INGREDIENTS

- 1 baguette
- 2 beefsteak tomatoes
- 1 clove garlic
- ¼ olive oil

DIRECTIONS

1. Toast the bread and cut the garlic clove
2. Rub with ½ half cut tomato to cover
3. Drizzle with oil and sprinkle with salt

Serves: 2
Prep Time: 5   Minutes

Cook Time: 15   Minutes

Total Time: 20   Minutes

INGREDIENTS

- 4 oz. spaghetti
- 2 cups basil leaves
- 2 garlic cloves
- ¼ cup olive oil
- 2 tablespoons parmesan cheese
- ½ tsp black pepper

DIRECTIONS

1. Bring water to a boil and add pasta
2. In a blend add parmesan cheese, basil leaves, garlic and blend
3. Add olive oil, pepper and blend again
4. Pour pesto onto pasta and serve when ready

ASPAGARUS WITH QUINCE JAM

Serves: **4**

Prep Time: **10**   Minutes

Cook Time: **30**   Minutes

Total Time: **40**   Minutes

INGREDIENTS

- 2 lb. asparagus spears
- 2 tablespoons fresh ginger
- 2 tablespoon quince jam
- 2 tablespoons olive oil
- 1 tsp lemon juice
- 2 tablespoons walnuts
- salt

DIRECTIONS

1. In a steamer add asparagus and steam until tender for 4-5 minutes
2. In a bowl whisk together, ginger, quince jam, olive oil, salt and lemon juice
3. Pour mixture over asparagus and sprinkle with walnuts

Serves: *2*
Prep Time: *10*   Minutes

Cook Time: *30*   Minutes

Total Time: *40*   Minutes

INGREDIENTS

- 2/4 lb mushrooms
- ¼ parmesan cheese
- salt
- arugula
- ¼ lb zucchini
- 3 tablespoons olive oil
- ¼ cup white wine
- 1 onion
- 1 cup brown rice
- 3 cups chicken broth
- 2 tablespoons parsley
- 1 garlic clover

DIRECTIONS

1. In a saucepan heat olive oil and add zucchini, mushrooms and season with salt
2. Cook for 2-3 minutes and transfer to a plate

3. Add onion, rice and wine and cook for 4-5 minutes
4. Add broth and mushrooms, garlic, zucchini and parsley
5. Transfer to a place and garnish with parmesan and arugula

GRASSFED BEEF & QUINOA CHILI

Serves: **6**

Prep Time: **10**   Minutes

Cook Time: **30**   Minutes

Total Time: **40**   Minutes

INGREDIENTS

- 1 onion
- 2 cloves garlic
- 1 lb. ground grassfed beef
- 1 tsp salt
- 1 tablespoon chili powder
- 1 tablespoon cumin
- 1 can diced tomatoes
- 1 can tomato sauce
- 1 cup water
- 2 cans kidney beans

DIRECTIONS

1. In a pot sauté onion and garlic until soft
2. Add spices, beef and chili powder
3. Stir in tomato sauce, tomatoes, beans and simmer for 15-20 minutes
4. When thickens remove from heat and serve with guacamole

TOMATO BASIL ORZO

Serves: **4**

Prep Time: **5**   Minutes

Cook Time: **15**   Minutes

Total Time: **20**   Minutes

INGREDIENTS

- 1 cup orzo pasta
- ¼ cup basil leaves
- ¼ cup sun-dried tomatoes
- 1 tablespoon olive oil
- ¼ cup parmesan cheese
- ¼ tsp salt
- ¼ tsp black pepper

DIRECTIONS

1. In a pot bring water to a boil, add orzo and cook for 10 minutes
2. In a blender add basil leaves, sun-dried tomatoes and blend until smooth
3. In a bowl toss together the orzo, and basil mixture with olive oil and parmesan cheese
4. Serve when ready

AVOCADO WRAPS

Serves: **2**

Prep Time: **10** Minutes

Cook Time: **20** Minutes

Total Time: **30** Minutes

INGREDIENTS

- 1 lb. pack chicken pieces
- ¼ tsp chili powder
- 1 garlic clove
- 1 tsp olive oil
- 2 wraps
- 1 avocado
- 1 roasted red pepper

DIRECTIONS

1. In a bowl combine chicken, chili powder, lime juice and garlic
2. In a pan heat oil and fry the chicken mixture
3. Add mixture to each wrap and top with avocado and red pepper

PENNE WITH AVOCADO

Serves: **4**

Prep Time: **10** Minutes

Cook Time: **20** Minutes

Total Time: **30** Minutes

INGREDIENTS

- 100g penne
- 1 tsp olive oil
- 1 onion
- 1 pepper
- 1 garlic clove
- 1 tsp chili powder
- 1 tsp coriander
- ¼ tsp cumin seeds
- 1 lb. tomatoes
- 1 can sweetcorn
- 1 avocado
- ¼ lime

DIRECTIONS

1. Cook the pasta for 10-15 minutes
2. In a pan heat oil and sautéed onion, garlic and tomatoes
3. Stir in water, corn and simmer for another 12-15 minutes

4. Toss the avocado with lime juice
5. Place the pasta in the pot, add remaining ingredients, cook for another 2-3 minutes
6. When ready remove from heat and serve

TUNA LETTUCE WRAPS

Serves: 2

Prep Time: *10*   Minutes

Cook Time: *15*   Minutes

Total Time: *25*   Minutes

INGREDIENTS

- 2 tuna fillets
- 1 avocado
- 1 tsp mustard powder
- 1 tsp apple cider vinegar
- 6 romaine lettuce leaves
- 8-10 cherry tomatoes

DIRECTIONS

1. In a pan add tuna and cook for 1-2 minutes per side
2. Combine avocado with vinegar, mustard powder and mix well
3. Spoon avocado mixture into lettuce leaves and top with tomatoes
4. When ready serve with tuna

VEGETABLE IDLI

Serves: 2

Prep Time: 5   Minutes

Cook Time: 25   Minutes

Total Time: 35   Minutes

INGREDIENTS

- ¼ cup toovar
- ¼ cup moong dal
- ¼ cup chana dal
- 1 cup fenugreek
- 1 cup coriander
- ½ cup green peas
- ½ cup coconut
- 2 green chillies
- ¼ cup onions
- ¼ cup carrot
- salt

DIRECTIONS

1. Soak the dals in water for 2-3 hours
2. Grind dals to paste, add the rest of the ingredients and mix well
3. Steam the paste for 12-15 minutes or until everything is tender

4. When ready remove from heat and serve

CUCUMBER CHANA DAL

Serves: 2

Prep Time: 5   Minutes

Cook Time: 20   Minutes

Total Time: 25   Minutes

INGREDIENTS

- ½ cup cucumber
- ½ cup chana dal
- 1 tsp cumin seeds
- ½ tsp chili powder
- 1 tsp turmeric powder
- 1 tsp olive oil

DIRECTIONS

1. Soak the chana dal in water for 1-2 hours
2. In a pan add cumin seeds and sauté for 1-2 minutes
3. Add the rest of the ingredients in the pan and cook for 12-15 minutes
4. When ready remove from heat and serve

OATS AND BROWN RICE

Serves: **4**

Prep Time: **10** Minutes

Cook Time: **30** Minutes

Total Time: **40** Minutes

INGREDIENTS

- ¼ cup oats
- ½ cup cooked brown rice
- 1 tablespoon moong dal
- 1 tsp olive oil
- ¼ cup onions
- 1 tsp garlic
- ¼ tsp ginger
- ½ cup beans
- ¼ cup carrot
- ¼ cup green peas
- 1 tablespoon coriander

DIRECTIONS

1. In a pressure cooker add onions, garlic, ginger and sauté for 2-3 minutes
2. Add green peas, beans, carrot and sauté for another 2-3 minutes

3. Add the rest of the ingredients, water and cook for another 5-6 minutes

4. Cook until the water has evaporated

5. When ready remove from heat and serve

AVOCADO DIP

Serves: **1**
Prep Time: **5**   Minutes

Cook Time: **5**   Minutes

Total Time: **10** Minutes

INGREDIENTS

- 1 cup avocado
- 1 tsp lemon juice
- 1 tablespoon tomatoes
- ¼ tsp green chillies
- salt

DIRECTIONS

1. In a blender combine all ingredients together
2. Blend until smooth
3. When ready remove and serve

BUCKWHEAT AND SPROUTS

Serves: 2

Prep Time: 5   Minutes

Cook Time: 20   Minutes

Total Time: 25   Minutes

INGREDIENTS

- ½ cup buckwheat
- ½ cup sprouts
- ½ cup moong dal
- 1 tsp olive oil
- 1 black peppercorn
- ¼ tsp cumin seeds
- 2 cloves
- ¼ tsp turmeric powder

DIRECTIONS

1. In a pressure cooker add cloves, cumin seeds and peppercorn, sauté for 2-3 minutes
2. Add the rest of the ingredients and water
3. Simmer for 12-15 minutes or until vegetables are soft
4. When ready remove from heat and serve

BROWN RICE

Serves: **4**

Prep Time: **10** Minutes

Cook Time: **40** Minutes

Total Time: **50** Minutes

INGREDIENTS

- 1 cup brown rice
- Salt
- 1 tsp olive oil

DIRECTIONS

1. Soak the brown rice in water for 30-40 minutes
2. When ready transfer to a pressure cooker
3. Cook for 6 whistles, when ready remove and serve

BROCCOLI SALAD

Serves: 2

Prep Time: 5   Minutes

Cook Time: 5   Minutes

Total Time: 10 Minutes

INGREDIENTS

- 1 cup broccoli
- 1 cup quinoa
- 2 radishes
- 2 tablespoons pumpkin seeds
- 1 cup salad dressing

DIRECTIONS

1. In a bowl combine all ingredients together and mix well
2. Serve with dressing

Serves: **2**
Prep Time: **5**   Minutes

Cook Time: **5**   Minutes

Total Time: **10**   Minutes

INGREDIENTS

- 1 cup cherry tomatoes
- 1 cucumber
- 1 cup olives
- ½ cup onion
- 1 cup feta
- 1 cup salad dressing

DIRECTIONS

1. In a bowl combine all ingredients together and mix well
2. Serve with dressing

POTATO SALAD

Serves: *2*

Prep Time: *5*   Minutes

Cook Time: *5*   Minutes

Total Time: *10* Minutes

INGREDIENTS

- 1 lb. white potatoes
- 4 slices bacon
- ½ red onion
- ¼ cup apple cider vinegar
- 1 tablespoon olive oil
- 4 green onions
- 1 tablespoon mustard

DIRECTIONS

1. In a bowl combine all ingredients together and mix well
2. Serve with dressing

Serves: **2**
Prep Time: **5**   Minutes

Cook Time: **5**   Minutes

Total Time: **10** Minutes

INGREDIENTS

- ¼ cup olive oil
- Juice of ½ lemon
- 2 avocados
- 1 cup cherry tomatoes
- ½ cup corn
- 1 tablespoon cilantro

DIRECTIONS

1. In a bowl combine all ingredients together and mix well
2. Serve with dressing

WATERMELON FETA SALAD

Serves: 2

Prep Time: 5   Minutes

Cook Time: 5   Minutes

Total Time: *10* Minutes

INGREDIENTS

- ¼ cup olive oi
- 1 tablespoon apple cider vinegar
- 2 cups watermelon
- 1 cup cucumber
- 1 cup feta
- ¼ cup red onion
- ¼ cup mint

DIRECTIONS

1. In a bowl combine all ingredients together and mix well
2. Serve with dressing

BACON JALAPENO SALAD

Serves: 2

Prep Time: 5 Minutes

Cook Time: 5 Minutes

Total Time: *10* Minutes

INGREDIENTS

- 2 cups corn
- 5 slices bacon
- 1 tablespoon cilantro
- 1 jalapeno
- ¼ cup mayonnaise
- 1 tsp chili powder
- 1 tsp garlic powder

DIRECTIONS

1. In a bowl combine all ingredients together and mix well
2. Serve with dressing

FISH STEW

Serves: **4**

Prep Time: **15**   Minutes

Cook Time: **45**   Minutes

Total Time: **60**   Minutes

INGREDIENTS

- 1 fennel bulb
- 1 red onion
- 2 garlic cloves
- 2 tablespoons olive oil
- 1 cup white wine
- 1 tablespoon fennel seeds
- 4 bay leaves
- 2 cups chicken stock
- 8 oz. halibut
- 12 oz. haddock

DIRECTIONS

1. Chop all ingredients in big chunks
2. In a large pot heat olive oil and add ingredients one by one
3. Cook for 5-6 or until slightly brown

4. Add remaining ingredients and cook until tender, 35-45 minutes
5. Season while stirring on low heat
6. When ready remove from heat and serve

BUTTERNUT SQUASH STEW

Serves: **4**

Prep Time: **15** Minutes

Cook Time: **45** Minutes

Total Time: **60** Minutes

INGREDIENTS

- 2 tablespoons olive oil
- 2 red onions
- 2 cloves garlic
- 1. Tablespoon rosemary
- 1 tablespoon thyme
- 2 lb. beef
- 1 cup white wine
- 1 cup butternut squash
- 2 cups beef broth
- ½ cup tomatoes
-

DIRECTIONS

1. Chop all ingredients in big chunks
2. In a large pot heat olive oil and add ingredients one by one
3. Cook for 5-6 or until slightly brown
4. Add remaining ingredients and cook until tender, 35-45 minutes

5. Season while stirring on low heat
6. When ready remove from heat and serve

ENCHILADA CASSEROLE

Serves: **4**

Prep Time: **10** Minutes

Cook Time: **25** Minutes

Total Time: **35** Minutes

INGREDIENTS

- 1 tablespoon olive oil
- 1 red onion
- 1 bell pepper
- 2 cloves garlic
- 1 can black beans
- 1 cup chicken
- 1 can green chilis
- 1 can enchilada sauce
- 1 cup cheddar cheese
- 1 cup sour cream

DIRECTIONS

1. Sauté the veggies and set aside
2. Preheat the oven to 425 F

3. Transfer the sautéed veggies to a baking dish, add remaining ingredients to the baking dish

4. Mix well, add seasoning and place the dish in the oven

5. Bake for 15-25 minutes or until slightly brown

6. When ready remove from the oven and serve

CHICKEN CASSEROLE

Serves: **4**

Prep Time: **10** Minutes

Cook Time: **15** Minutes

Total Time: **25** Minutes

INGREDIENTS

- 1 tablespoon olive oil
- 1 lb. chicken breast
- 1 red onion
- 2 cloves garlic
- 1 tsp paprika
- 4 cups cooked rice
- ¼ cup cranberries
- 1 lb. brussels sprouts
- 1 potato

DIRECTIONS

1. Sauté the veggies and set aside
2. Preheat the oven to 425 F
3. Transfer the sautéed veggies to a baking dish, add remaining ingredients to the baking dish
4. Mix well, add seasoning and place the dish in the oven
5. Bake for 12-15 minutes or until slightly brown

6. When ready remove from the oven and serve

CASSEROLE PIZZA

Serves: *6-8*

Prep Time: *10*   Minutes

Cook Time: *15*   Minutes

Total Time: *25*   Minutes

INGREDIENTS

- 1 pizza crust
- ½ cup tomato sauce
- ¼ black pepper
- 1 cup zucchini slices
- 1 cup mozzarella cheese
- 1 cup olives

DIRECTIONS

5. Spread tomato sauce on the pizza crust
6. Place all the toppings on the pizza crust
7. Bake the pizza at 425 F for 12-15 minutes
8. When ready remove pizza from the oven and serve

THANK YOU FOR READING THIS BOOK!

CPSIA information can be obtained
at www.ICGtesting.com
Printed in the USA
BVHW031352150321
602550BV00001B/143